AA

· GLOVEBOX ATLAS ·
TOWN PLANS
OF BRITAIN

2nd edition April 1994
1st edition April 1992

© The Automobile Association 1994

The Automobile Association retains the copyright in the
original edition © 1992 and in all subsequent editions
reprints and amendments to editions listed above.

Published by AA Publishing (a tradename of Automobile Association
Developments Ltd, whose registered office is Norfolk House, Priestley
Road, Basingstoke, Hampshire RG24 9NY. Registered number 1878835) .

Standard ISBN 0 7495 0876 0
Spiral   ISBN 0 7495 0877 9

Mapping produced by the Cartographic Department of
The Automobile Association

Printed by BPC Paulton Books, Paulton.

The contents of this book are believed correct at the time
of printing. Nevertheless, the publishers cannot be held responsible
for any errors or omissions or for changes in the details given.

A CIP catalogue record for this book is available from the
British Library

(iii)

Map Symbols

AA recommended roads	
Other roads	
Restricted roads	
Buildings of interest	Museum
Car Parks	P
Parks and open spaces	
Churches	+
One way streets	

CONTENTS

Town plan location map and map symbols
(iii)

Town Plans
2-123

Mileage Chart
124

Town Plans

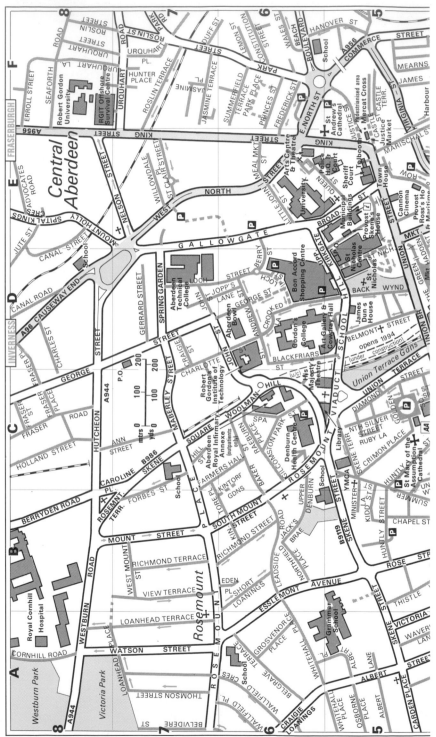

ABERDEEN

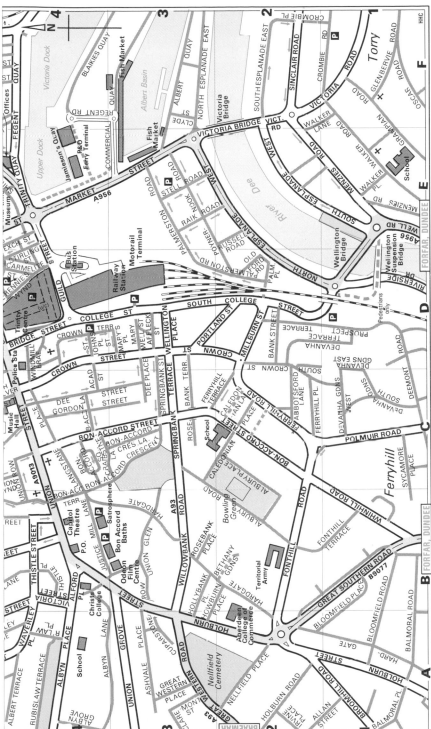

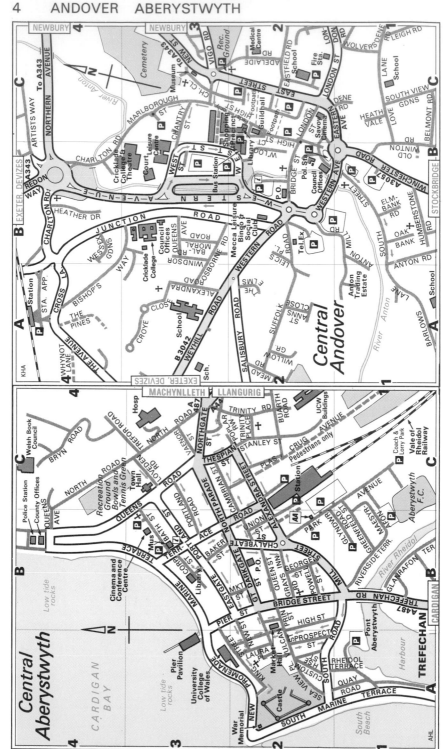

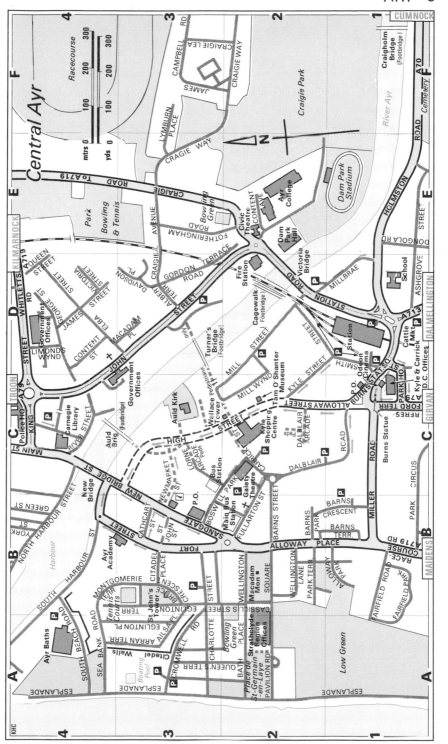

Central Ayr

AYR

BATH

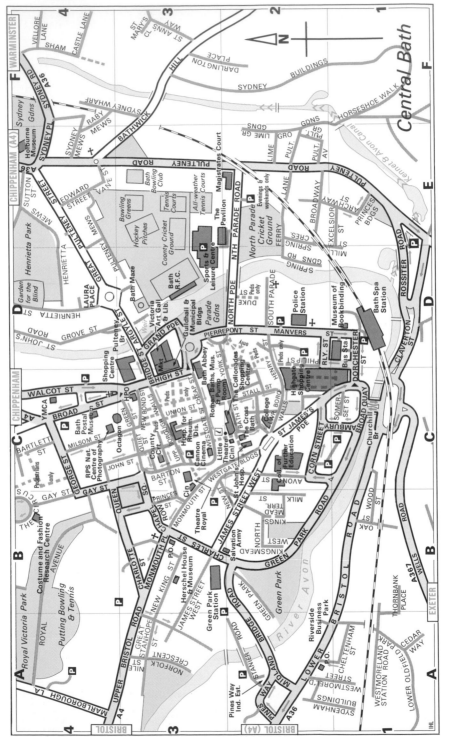

Central Bath

BLACKPOOL

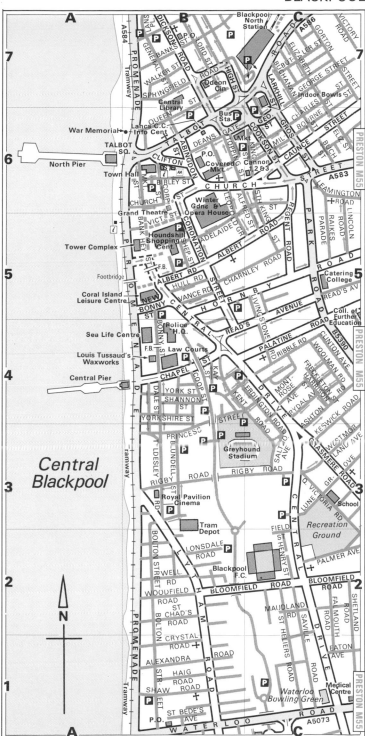

Central Blackpool

BIRMINGHAM

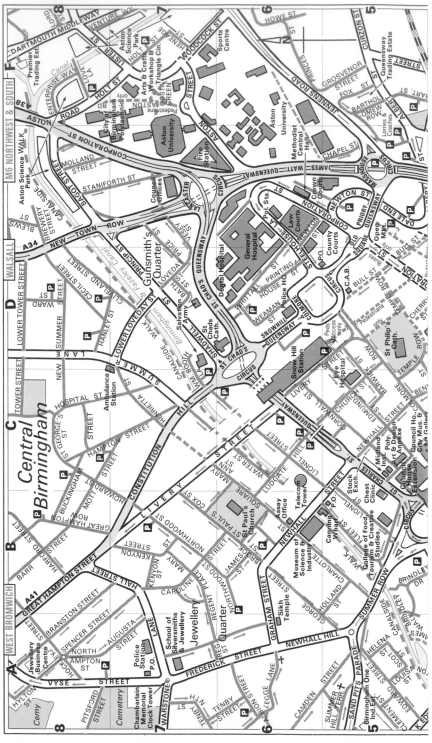

BIRMINGHAM

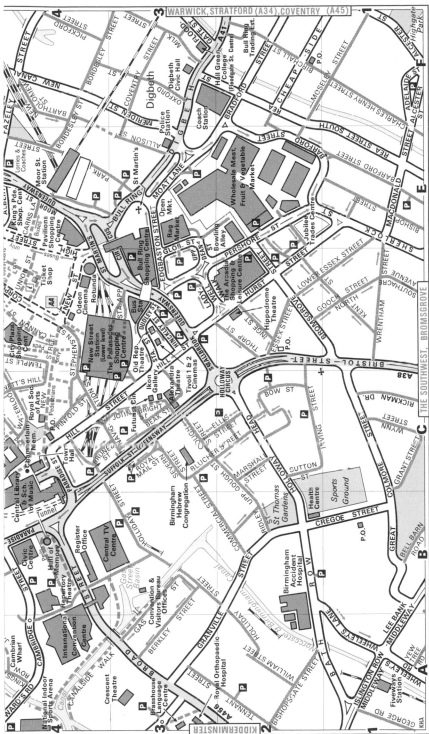

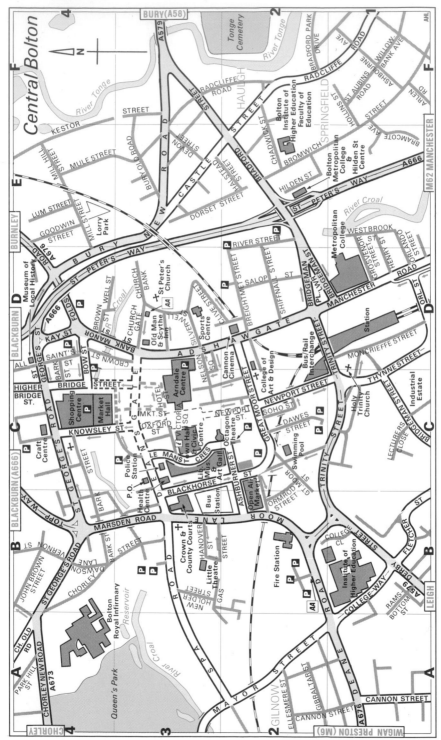

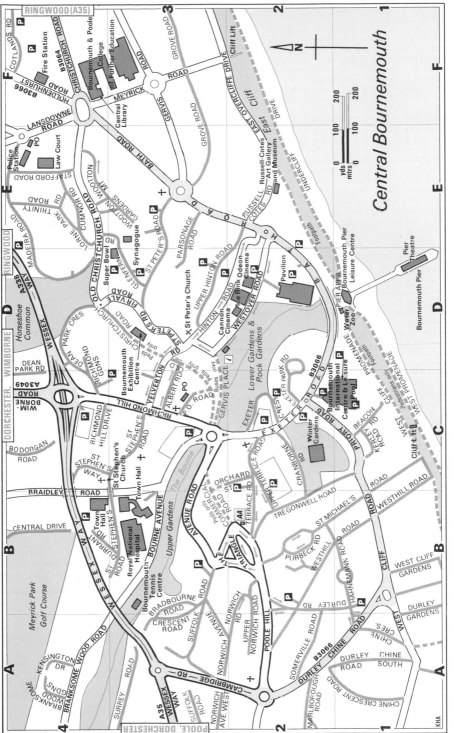

BOURNEMOUTH

Central Bournemouth

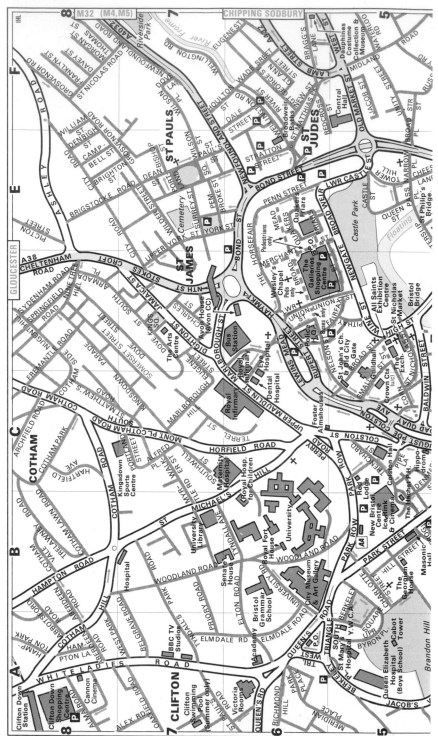

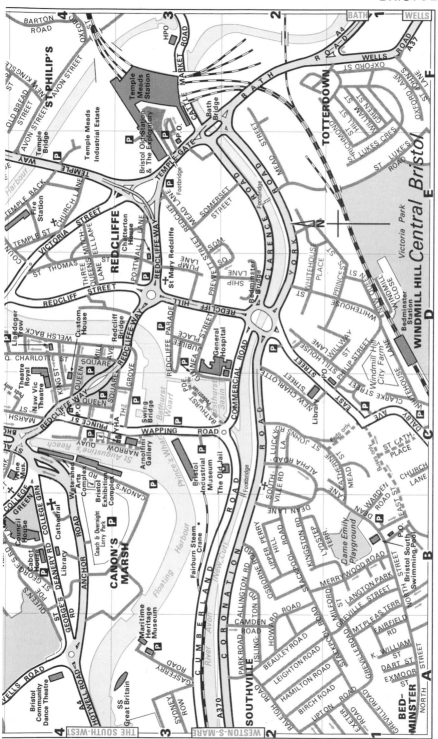

BATH
WELLS
HPO
BARTON ROAD
OXFORD ST
ST PHILIP'S
NEW KINGSLEY
OLD BREAD STREET
AVON STREET
ST
AVON STREET
Temple Meads Station
CATTLE MARKET ROAD
BATH
WELLS ROAD
A4
A37
OXFORD ST
OXFORD LANE
ST JOHNS LANE
Bath Bridge
TOTTERDOWN
RICHMOND ST
WILLIAM ST
GREEN ST
ST LUKES CRES
ST LUKE'S ROAD
Temple Bridge
Temple Meads Industrial Estate
Bristol Old Station & The Exploratory
TEMPLE WAY
TEMPLEGATE
P.O.
Footbridge
SOMERSET STREET
MEAD STREET
CLARENCE ROAD
YORK ROAD
Footbridge
Victoria Park
Central Bristol
Fire Station
TEMPLE BACK
Harbour
TEMPLE ST
COUNT
VICTORIA STREET
CHURCH LANE
REDCLIFFE STREET
MITCH-ELL LANE
Chatterton House
REDCLIFFE WAY
ST Mary Redcliffe
PUMP LANE
SHIP LANE
SOM. SQ.
PREWETT STREET
Bedminster Bridge
WHITEHOUSE ST
WHITEHOUSE PLACE
PRINCES ST
STILLHOUSE LANE
Bedminster Station
WINDMILL HILL
Windmill Hill City Farm
WINDMILL CLOSE
ST THOMAS ST
THREE QUEENS LANE
PORTWALL LANE
REDCLIFF HILL
CLARKE STREET
WHITEHOUSE LANE
REDCLIFF STREET
Custom House
Redcliff Bridge
P
REDCLIFFE PARADE
JUBILEE PLACE
LINEA
General Hospital
PDE.
COMMERCIAL ROAD
NEW CHARLOTTE STREET
EAST STREET
Library
P.O.
ST PHILIP STREET
DALBY AVE
Llandoger Trow
WELSH BACK
Q. CHARLOTTE ST
QUEEN SQUARE
MILL AVE
THE GROVE
BATHURST Wharf
Bathurst Basin
WILLWAY ST
SOUTH VILLE RD
DEAN LANE
WARDEN RD
EAST ST
ST CATH. PLACE
CHURCH LANE
Theatre Royal
New Vic Theatre
KING ST
PRINCE ST
QUEEN ST
REDCLIFFE WAY
Swing Bridge
WAPPING ROAD
Arnolfini Gallery
Bristol Industrial Museum
The Old Gaol
Footbridge
LUCKY LA
ST JOHNS RD
ALPHA ROAD
DEAN LANE
LYDSTEP TERR
Dame Emily Playground
MERRY WOOD ROAD
Bristol South Swimming Pool
MARSH ST
Reach
St Augustine's
NARROW QUAY
Prince's Wharf
Harbour
Floating
New Cut
ALLINGTON RD
UPPER PERRY HILL
STACKPOOL ROAD
KINGSTON RD
NORTH STREET
P.O.
LANGTON PARK
GREVILLE STREET
Wine Mus.
COLLEGE GREEN
Council House
Cabot House
Cathedral
Library
DEANERY RD
ANCHOR ROAD
CANON'S ROAD
Watershed Arts Complex
Bristol Exhibition Complex
Coach & Overnight Lorry Park
CANON'S MARSH
Fairburn Steam Crane
CUMBERLAND ROAD
CORONATION ROAD
CAMDEN ROAD
SOUTHVILLE
PARK ROAD
ISLING-
HOWARD RD
OSBORNE ROAD
BEAULEY ROAD
LEIGHTON ROAD
HAMILTON ROAD
MILFORD ST
GREVILLE STREET
MT PLEAS.TERR
FAIRFIELD RD
K. WILLIAM ST
DART ST
EXMOOR ST
WILLS ROAD
HOTWELL ROAD
A4
Bristol Community Dance Theatre
QUEEN'S PDE.
ST GEORGE'S RD
GEORGE'S RD
Maritime Heritage Museum
SS Great Britain
GASFERRY ROAD
SYDNEY ROW
River Avon
BIRCH ROAD
UPTON ROAD
RALEIGH ROAD
EXETER ROAD
GREVILLE ROAD
NORTH STREET
BED-MINSTER
WELLS ROAD

THE SOUTH-WEST
WESTON-S-MARE

N

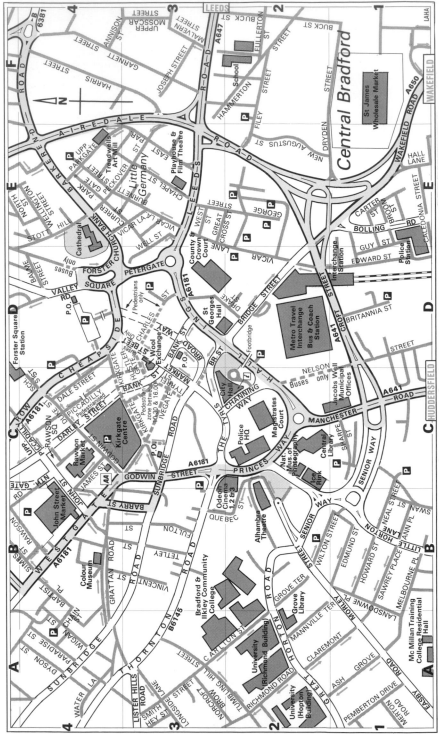

BRIGHTON

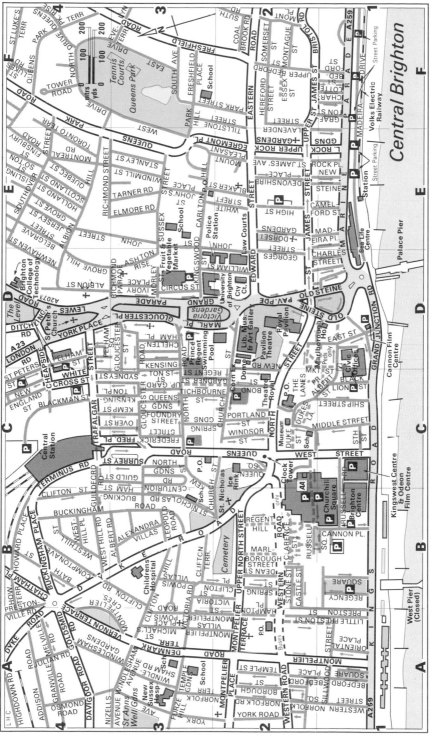

Central Brighton

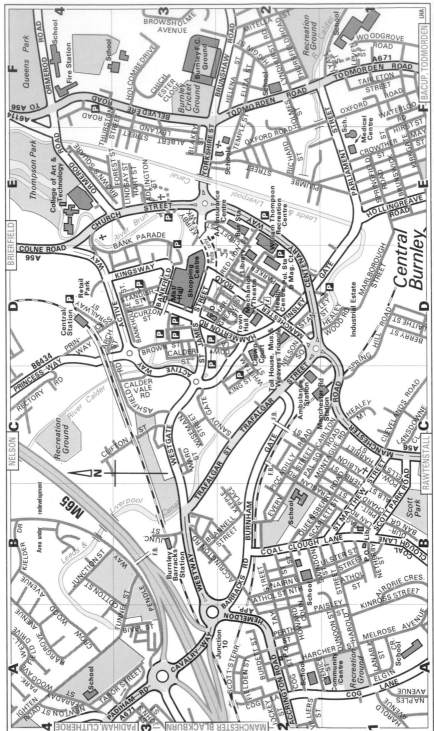

BURNLEY

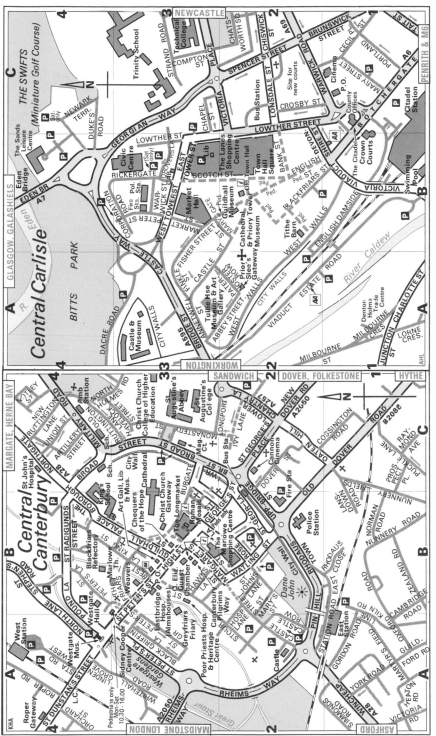

CANTERBURY   CARLISLE

Carlisle map

Central Carlisle

THE SWIFTS
(Miniature Golf Course)

The Sands Leisure Centre

Eden Bridge
EDEN BR
R. Eden

GLASGOW, GALASHIELS

BITTS PARK

DACRE ROAD

Castle & Museum
CITY WALLS

NEWARK TERR.
DUKE'S ROAD

GEORGIAN WAY

Civic Centre
RICKERGATE
CORPORATION ROAD

CASTLE WAY

BRIDGEWELL ST
FINKLE ST
FISHER STREET
PETER ST
WEST WALLS
ABBEY STREET

A595 ST

WEST TOWER ST
MARKET ST
CASTLE ST
PATER ST

LOWTHER ST
SCOTCH ST
CASTLE ST

Market Hall

Pol. Sta.
Fire Sta.
WAR. WICK ST
Sat only

NEWCASTLE

Technical College
Trinity School
STRAND ROAD
COMPTON ST
VICTORIA PLACE
CHAPEL ST

SPENCER STREET
CHATS WORTH ST
A69
CHISWICK ST
WORTH ST

Bus Station
ONSDALE ST

Site for new courts
Cinema
P.O.
County Offices
CROSBY ST

BRUNSWICK STREET
CECIL ST
MARY STREET
PORTLAND
A6
TAIT ST

LOWTHER STREET

The Lanes Shopping Centre
Lib
TOWER ST
Town Hall
Town Hall Square
BANK ST
WARWICK ST
ENGLISH ST
DEVON SHIRE ST

AA
Crown Courts
The Citadel
Citadel Station

PENRITH & M6

Cathedral
Prior Slee's Gateway
& Priory Tower
Museum
Guildhall Museum
BLACKFRIARS ST
ENGLISH DAMSIDE
ESTATE ROAD
VIADUCT

Tithe Barn

CITY WALLS
WEST WALLS

River Caldew

Denton Holme Trade Centre
MILBOURNE CRES.
LORNE CRES.
JUNCTION ST
CHARLOTTE ST
MILBOURNE ST
AA

Swimming Pool

VICTORIA VIADUCT
BOTCHERGATE

Canterbury map

Central Canterbury

MARGATE, HERNE BAY

MOTLEY RD
NEW RUTTINGTON LANE
UNION ST
NORTHGATE
A28
ROPER ROAD
LINDEN GROVE
ST DUNSTANS STREET
ORCHARD ST
L.C.
WHITEHALL ROAD

NORTH HOLMES RD
HAVELOCK ST
MILITARY ROAD
ARTILLERY STREET
BROAD STREET

St John's Hospital
Roper Gateway
West Station
Westgate Mus.
Sidney Cooper Centre
Westgate Hall
Westgate Gardens
BLACK GRIFFIN LA
ST PETER'S GROVE
Greyfriars Friary
Eastbridge Hosp. & Almshouses
POUND LANE
Blackfriars Refectory
Marlowe Th.
KING ST
STOUR ST
GUILDHALL ST
HIGH ST
MERCERY LA

Christ Church College of Higher Education
St Augustine's Abbey
St Augustine's College
City Wall
MONASTERY ST
LONGPORT
BROAD ST
Mag. Ct.
Bus Sta

Art Gall, Lib & Mus.
Chequers
Christ Church Gateway
Cathedral of the Hope
The Longmarket
Roman Mosaic
King's School
Sch.
BURGATE
BUTCHERY LA
LOWER BR ST
ST GEORGE'S PLACE
NEW DOVER RD
A2050

SANDWICH
DOVER, FOLKESTONE
HYTHE

COSSINGTON ROAD
DOVER STREET
OATEN HILL
NUNNERY FIELDS
PUCKLE LANE
PROS. PECT. PL.
RAY-MOND AVE
B2088

Cannon Cinema
Fire Sta
Police Station
Dane John
East Station
STATION ROAD EAST CLOSE
Canterbury Heritage Centre
Poor Priests Hosp. & Heritage Centre
Pilgrims Way
Marlowe Shopping Centre
Chamber
Weavers
Guest
P.O.
Eliz.
WATLING ST
ST GEORGE'S ST
CASTLE ST
GAS ST
HAWKS LANE
ST MARGARET'S ST
ST JOHN'S LANE
HOSP. LANE
ST MARY'S
CANTERBURY LA
PIN HILL
RHODAUS TOWN
RHODAUS TOWN
City Wall
UPR BRIDGE ST
LOWER BRIDGE ST
OLD DOVER ROAD

NORMAN ROAD
NUNNERY ROAD
CAMBRIDGE ROAD
ZEALAND RD
LIME KILN RD
OXFORD RD
GORDON ROAD
GUILD. FORD RD
HEATON RD
YORK ROAD
WINCHEAP
A28
VICTORIA RD
SIMMONDS ROAD

RHEIMS WAY
A2050
MAIDSTONE LONDON
ASHFORD
Great Stour

KHA
AHL

CAMBRIDGE

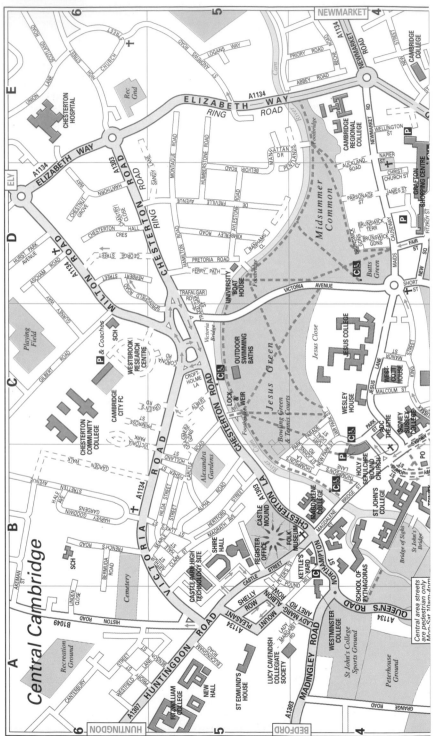

Central Cambridge

NEWMARKET

Central area streets are pedestrian only Mon.-Sat. 10am-4pm

CAMBRIDGE

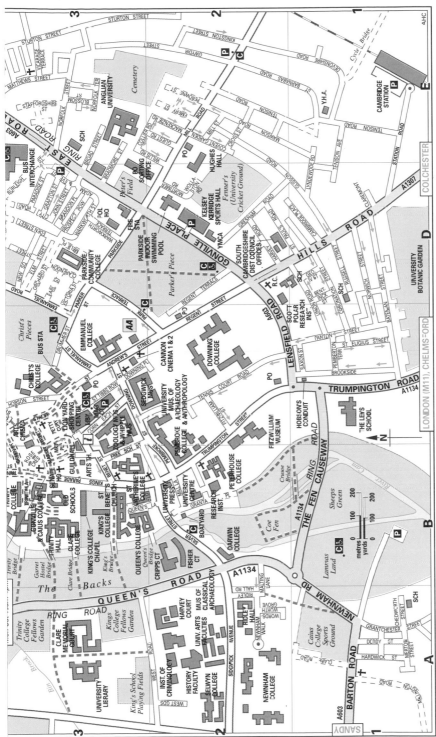

CARDIFF

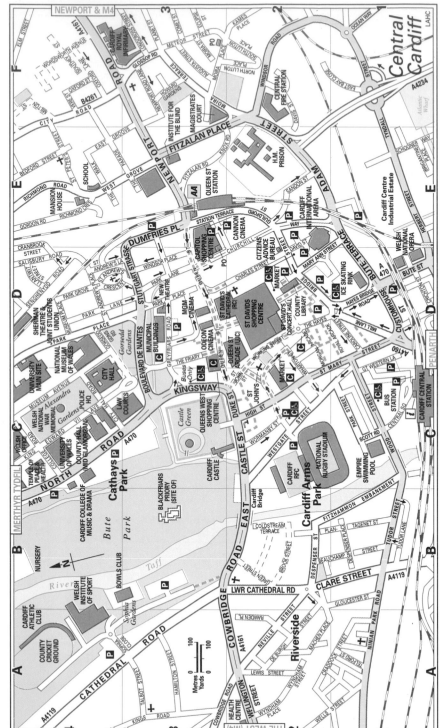

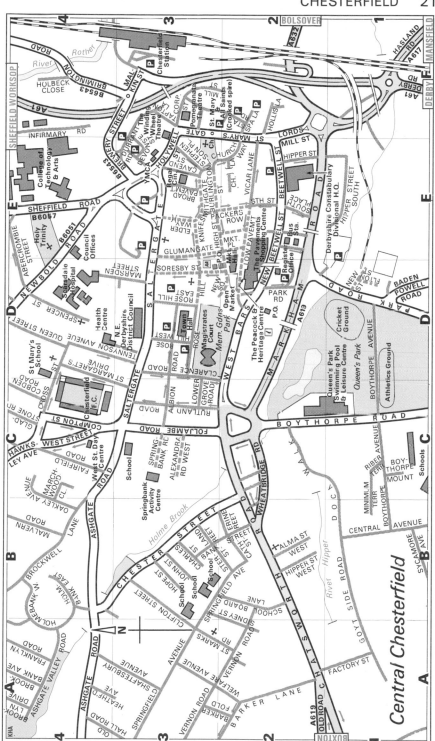

CHESTERFIELD

Central Chesterfield

CHELMSFORD

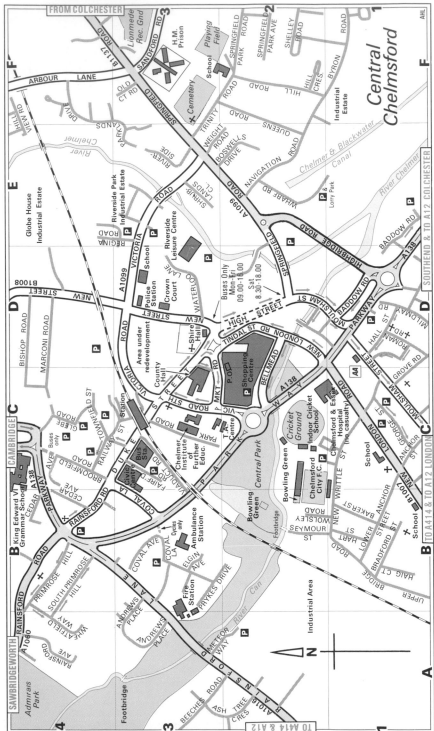

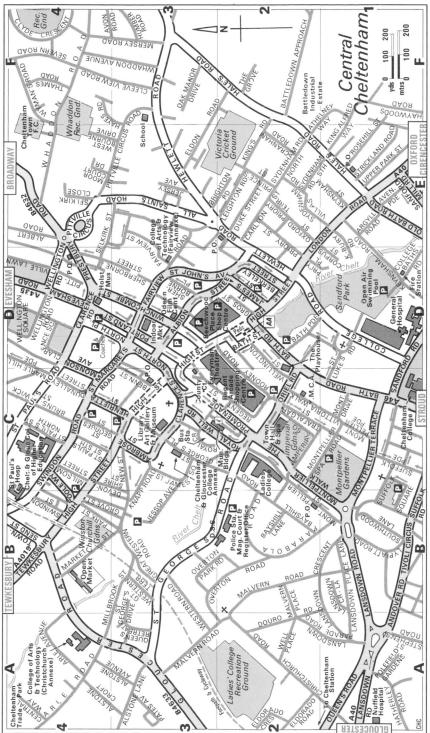

CHELTENHAM

Central Cheltenham

CHESTER

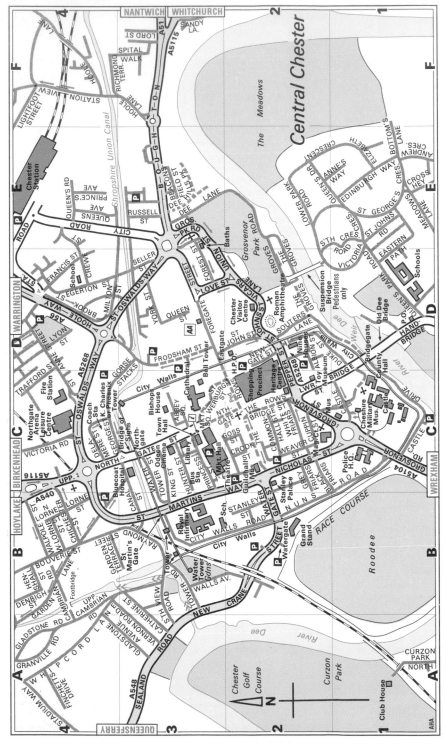

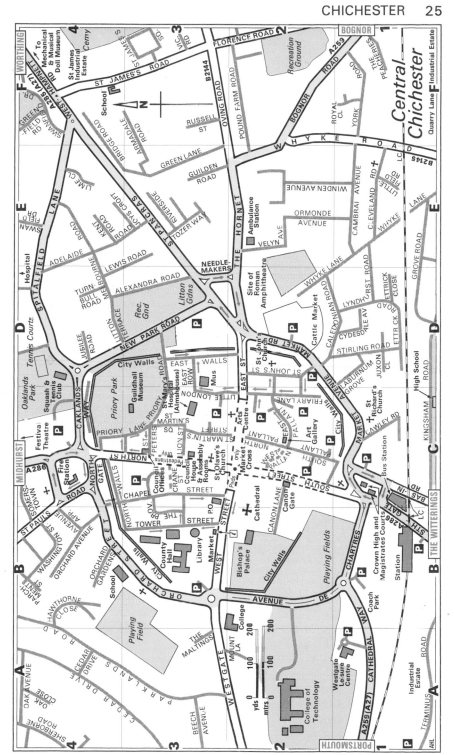

Central Chichester

COLCHESTER

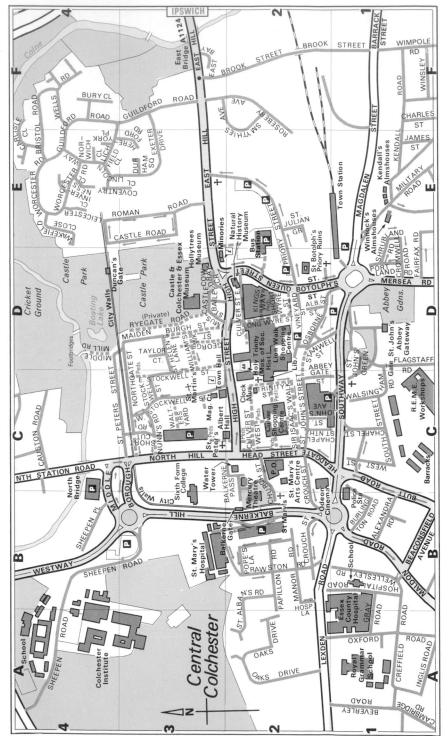

Central Colchester

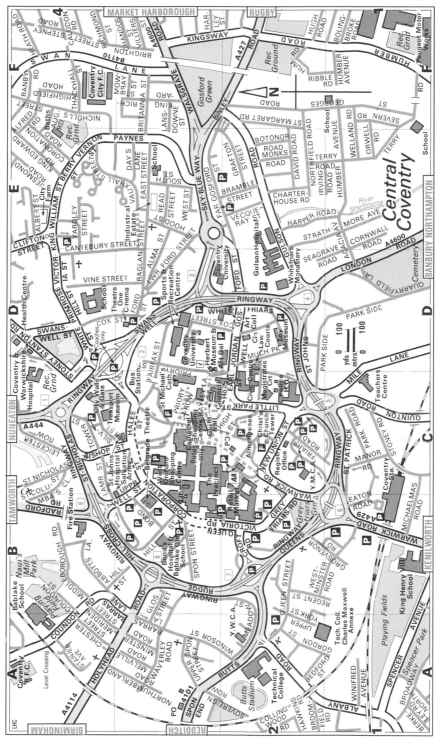

COVENTRY

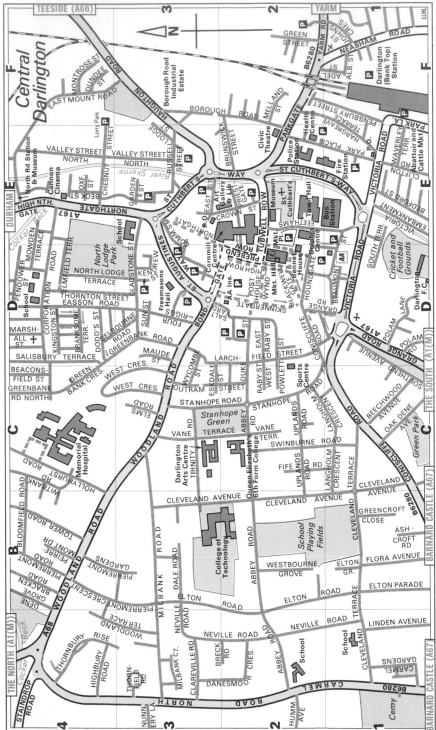

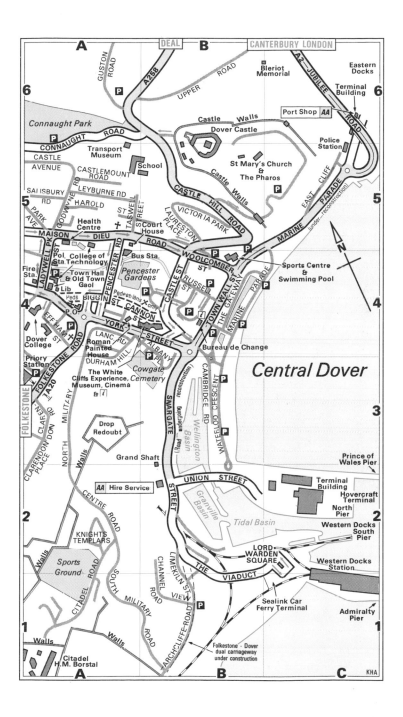

Central Dover

DERBY

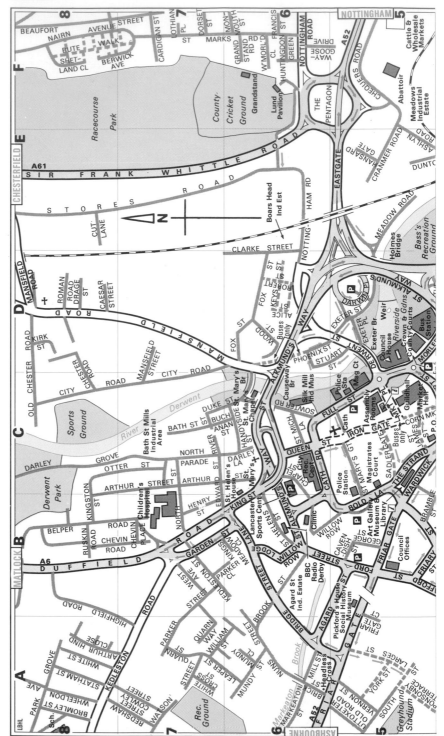

DERBY

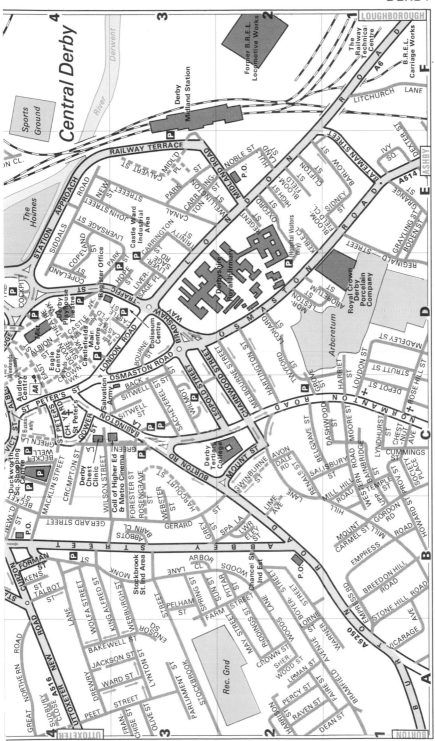

Central Derby

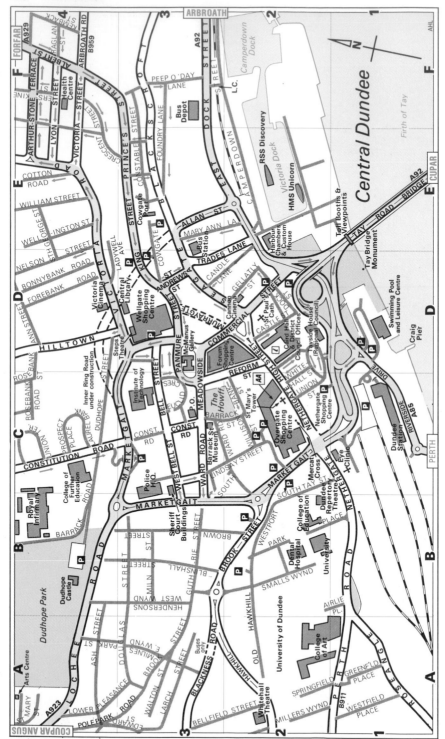

DUNDEE

Central Dundee

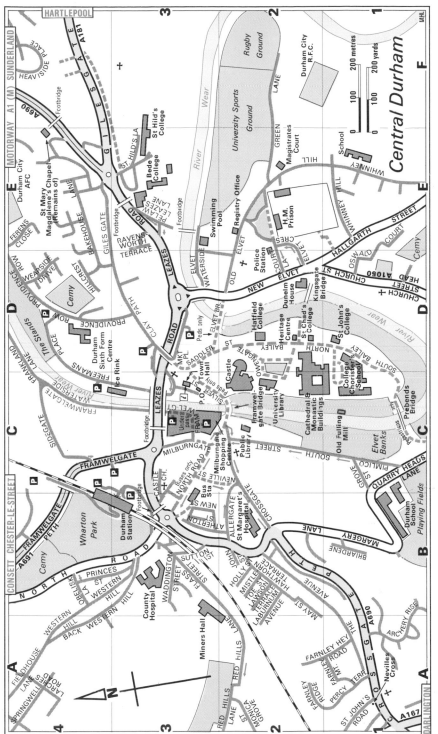

DURHAM

Central Durham

HARTLEPOOL
A181
GILLESGATE
A690 MOTORWAY A1 (M) SUNDERLAND
HEAVISIDE PLACE
Footbridge
Durham City AFC
St Mary Magdalene's Chapel (Remains of)
FEBENS CLOSE
WEARSIDE DRIVE
BAKEHOUSE
GILES GATE
ST. HILD'S LA.
St Hild's College
Bede College
PELAW LEAZES LANE
RAVENSWORTH TERRACE
HILLCREST
Cemy
Cemy
PROVIDENCE ROW
The Stands
FRANKLAND LANE
PLACE
FREEMANS
Ice Rink
Durham Sixth Form Centre
CLAY PATH
LEAZES ROAD
Footbridge
Footbridge
River Wear
Swimming Pool
Registry Office
ELVET
WATERSIDE
Elvet Br.
Peds only
University Sports Ground
Rugby Ground
Durham City R.F.C.
GREEN LANE
Magistrates Court
HILL
WHINNEY HILL
School
Police Station
OLD ELVET
NEW ELVET
ELVET CRES.
ELVET LA.
H.M. Prison
HALLGARTH STREET
CHURCH STREET
CHURCH STREET HEAD
A1050
Cemy
COURT
WHINNEY HILL
Hatfield College
Heritage Centre
St Chad's College
Kingsgate Bridge
St John's College
River Wear
Dunelm House
SADDLER ST
OWENGATE
NORTH BAILEY
SOUTH BAILEY
College
Chorister's School
Castle
Town Hall
MKT PL.
SILVER ST.
P.O.
Peds only
Framwelgate Bridge
University Library
Cathedral & Monastic Buildings
Prebends Bridge
Old Fulling Mill
Elvet Banks
LEAZES
FRAM.
Underpass
Footbridge
MILBURNGATE
FRAMWELGATE
NORTH ROAD
CASTLE CH.
Milburngate Shopping Centre
Public Library
NEVILLE ST.
Bus Sta
Buses only
NEW ST
ST MARGARET'S
St Margaret's Hospital
ALLERGATE
CROSSGATE
SOUTH STREET
GROVE
PIMLICO
QUARRY HEADS LANE
Durham School
Playing Fields
BRIARDENE
MARGERY LANE
CONSETT CHESTER-LE-STREET
A691
FRAMWELGATE PETH
Wharton Park
Cemy
NORTH ROAD
Durham Station
Footbridge
ATHERTON ST
SUTTON ST
FLASS STREET
WADDINGTON ST
PRINCES ST
OBELISK LA.
WESTERN HILL
County Hospital
BACK WESTERN HILL
WESTERN HILL
FIELDHOUSE LANE
LARCHES ROAD
SPRINGWELL AVE
Miners Hall
RED HILLS
RED HILLS LANE
JOHN ST
HOLLY ST
HAWTHORN TERRACE
MISTLETOE ST
FOREST RD
LAWSON TERRACE
LABURNUM AVENUE
MAY ST
MONICA GROVE
FARNLEY RIDGE
PERCY TERR.
FARNLEY HEY ROAD
FARNLEY MT.
THE AVENUE
A690
THE GROVE
CROSSGATE PETH
ST JOHN'S ROAD
ARCHERY RISE
Nevilles Cross
DARLINGTON A167

200 metres
200 yards
100
100
0

N

F E D C B A
1 2 3 4

EASTBOURNE

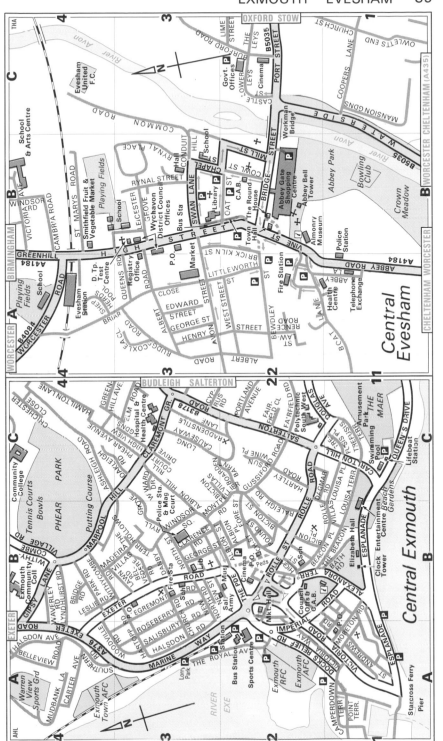

EXMOUTH EVESHAM

EDINBURGH

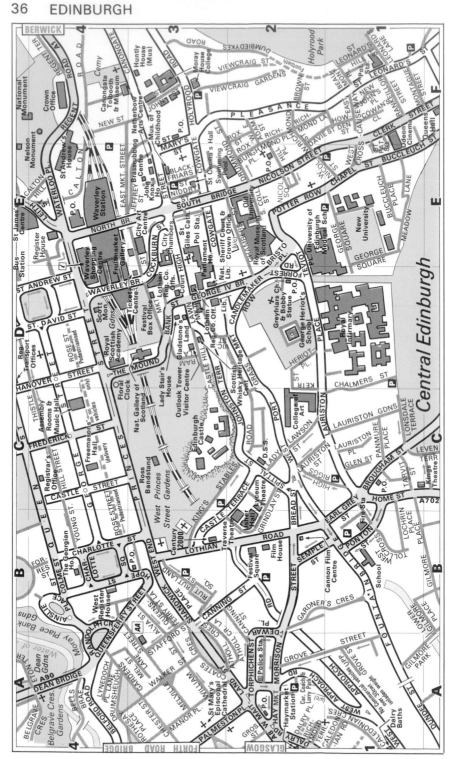

Central Edinburgh

ENFIELD

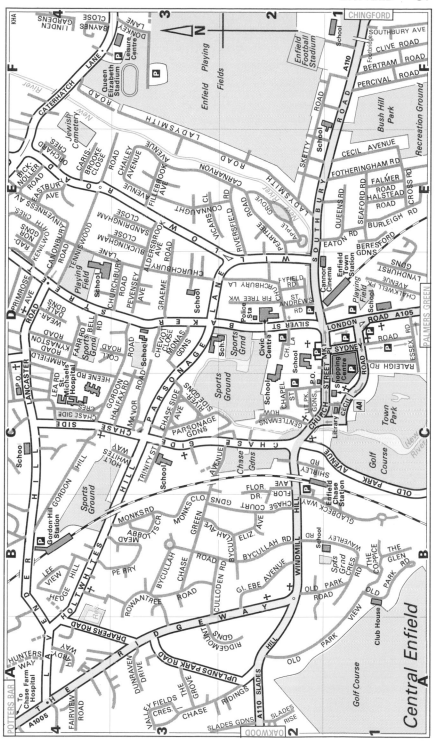

Central Enfield

EXETER

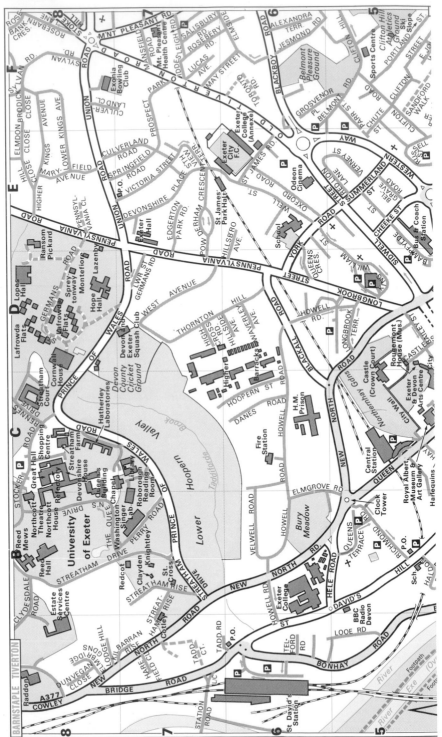

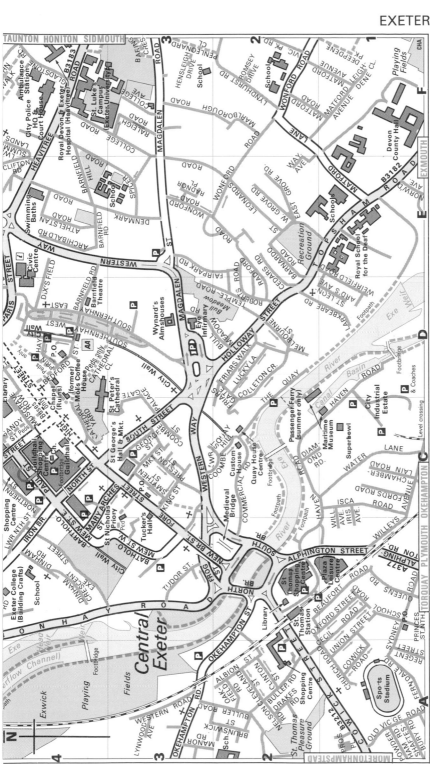

FARNBOROUGH   FELIXSTOWE

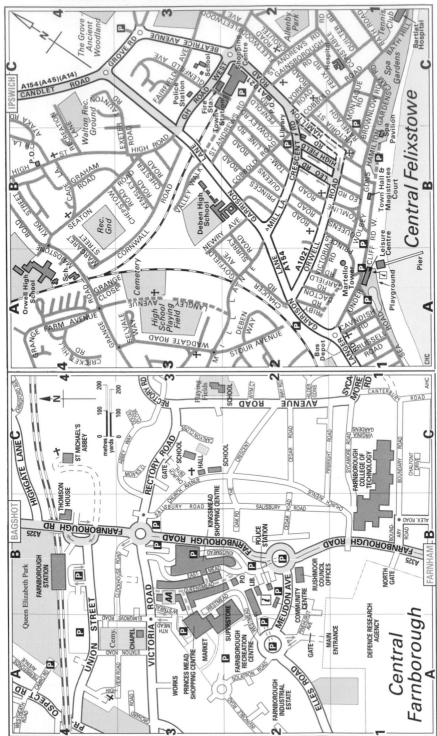

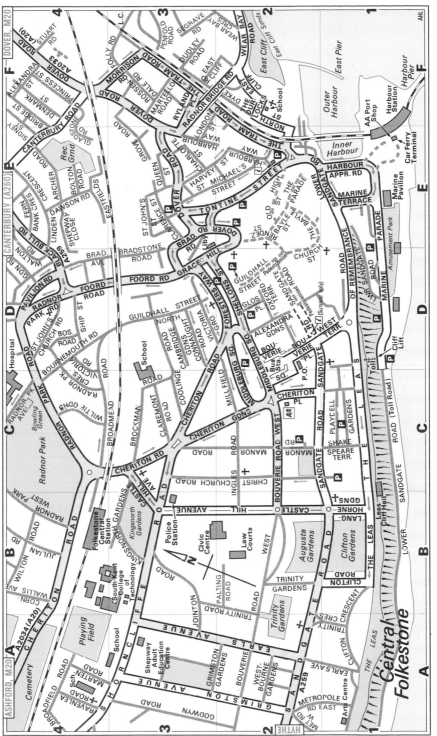

GLOUCESTER

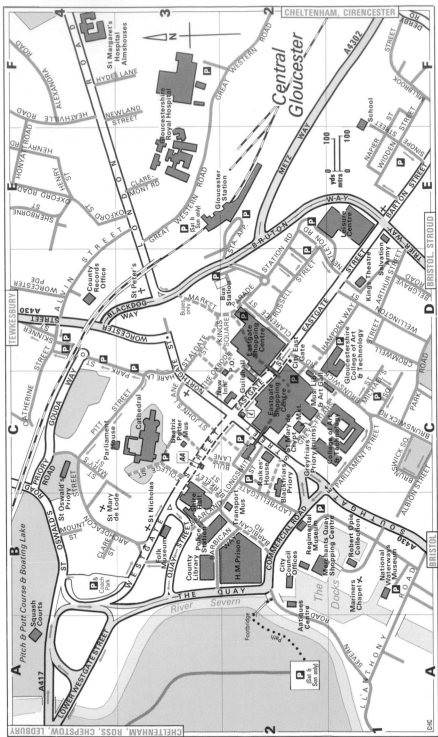

CHELTENHAM, CIRENCESTER

Central Gloucester

St Margaret's Hospital Almshouses

Gloucestershire Royal Hospital

Gloucester Station

School

County Records Office

Leisure Centre

Kings Theatre

Salvation Army

Bus Station

Eastgate Shopping Centre

City East Gate

Gloucestershire College of Art & Technology

Cathedral

Beatrix Potter Mus

New Inn

Guildhall

EASTGATE

Mus. Library & Art Gall

Eastgate Shopping Centre

St Mary de Crypt Mkt.

College of Art & Technology

Parliament House

St Mary de Lode

St Nicholas

Greyfriars St Mary de Crypt Priory (ruins)

Raikes House

Blackfriars Priory

Shire Hall

Folk Museum

Police Station

County Library

Transport Mus

H.M. Prison

Regimental Museum

City Council Offices

Merchants Quay Shopping Centre

Robert Opie Collection

National Waterways Museum

Mariners Chapel

The Docks

Squash Courts

P & Coach Park

THE QUAY

River Severn

Footbridge

Path

Antiques Centre

Pitch & Putt Course & Boating Lake

CHELTENHAM, ROSS, CHEPSTOW, LEDBURY

TEWKESBURY A430

BRISTOL, STROUD

BRISTOL

GILLINGHAM   GRIMSBY

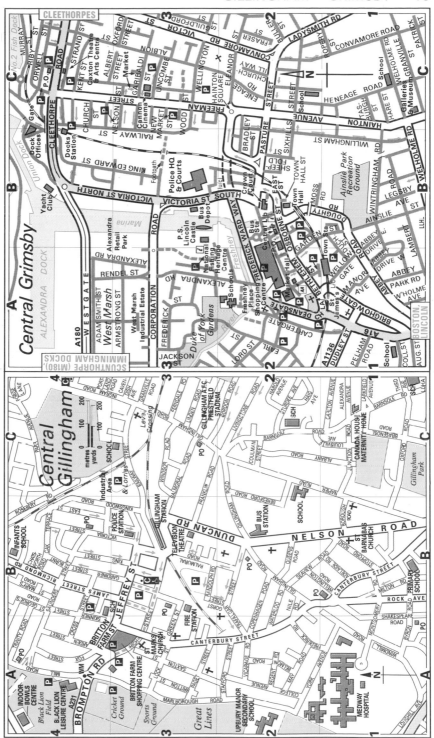

GLASGOW

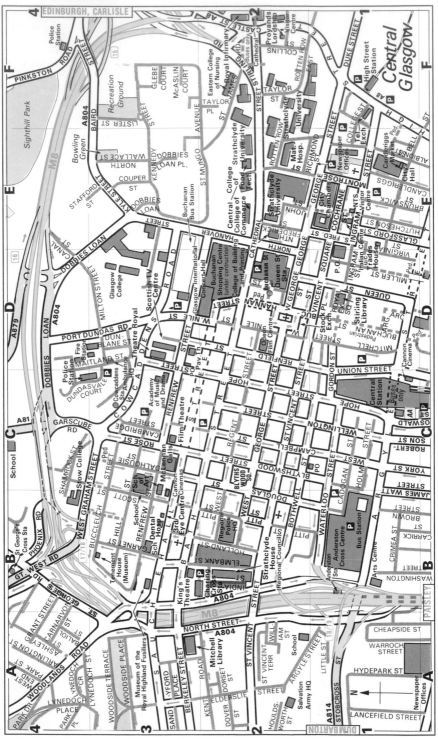

GUILDFORD

Central Guildford

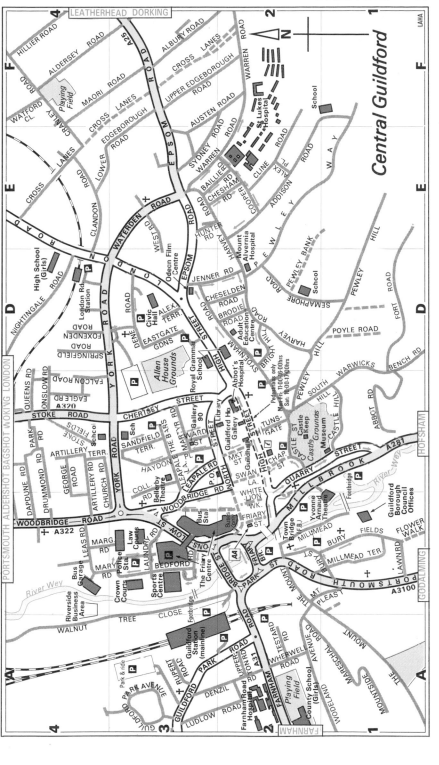

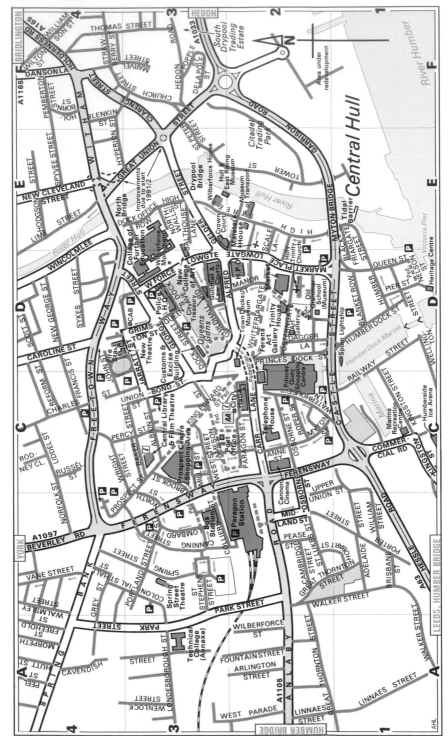

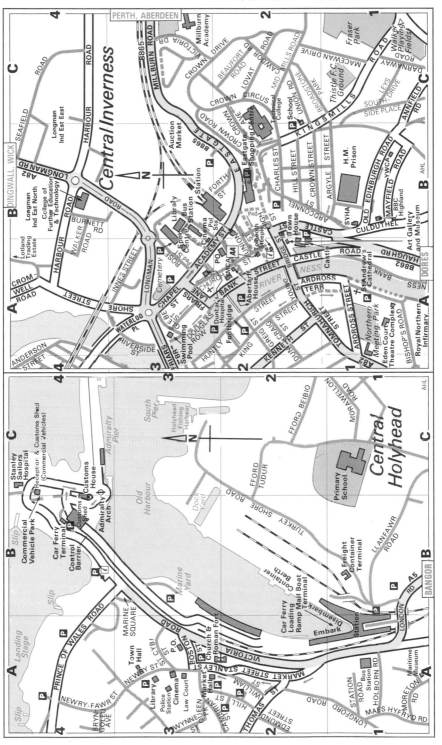

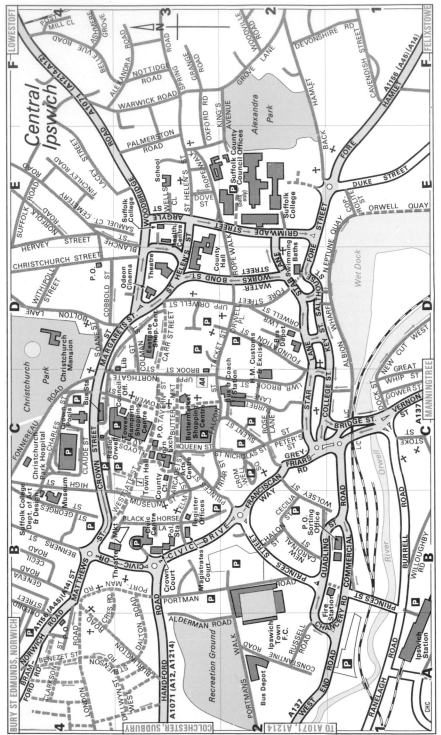

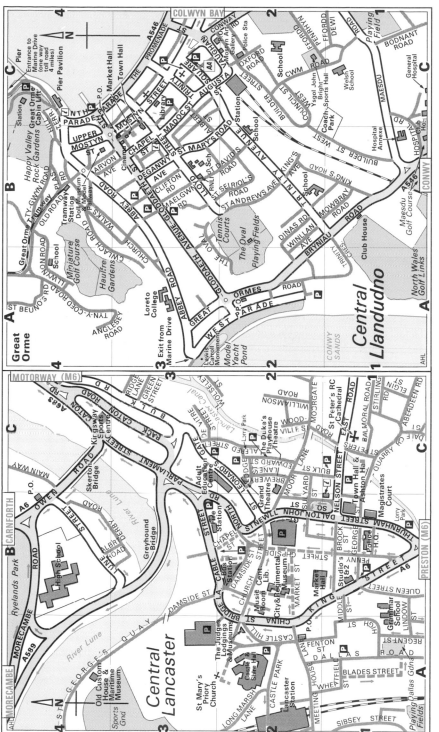

LANCASTER LLANDUDNO

LEEDS

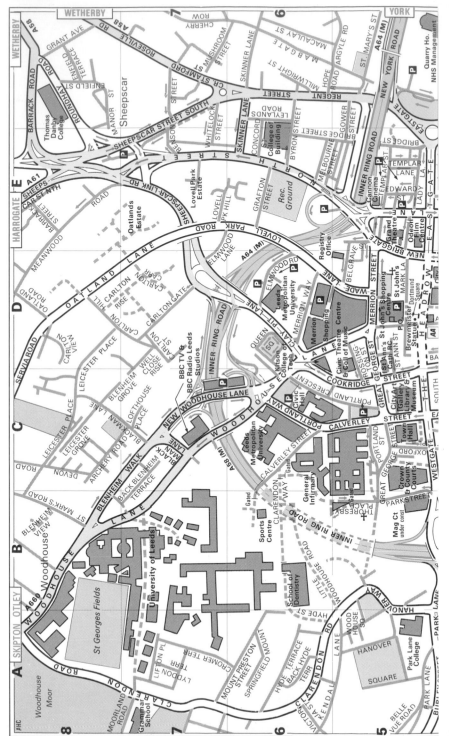

LEEDS

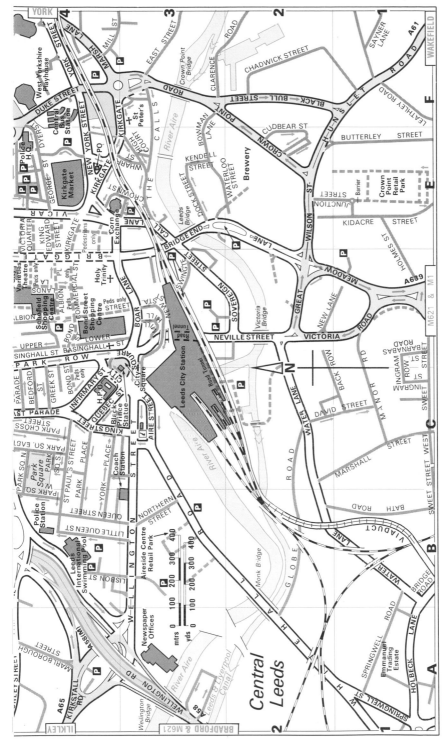

YORK

4 3 2 1

West Yorkshire Playhouse

DUKE STREET

MARSH LANE

YORK STREET

MILL ST

EAST STREET

ROAD

CROWN POINT BRIDGE

CHADWICK STREET

CLARENCE ROAD

SAYNER LANE

A61 ROAD WAKEFIELD

Central Bus Station

NEW YORK STREET

KIRKGATE

St Peter's

HIGH CT

WHARF ST

ROAD

BLACK BULL STREET

CROWN POINT

HUNSLET

LEATHLEY ROAD

F

Police HQ

GEORGE ST

DYER'S

Kirkgate Market

PO

KIRKGATE

THE CALLS

River Aire

BONMANI LANE

CUDBEAR ST

WILSON ST

BREWERY

BUTTERLEY STREET

KENDELL STREET

WATERLOO STREET

Leeds Bridge

DOCK STREET

JUNCTION STREET

Barrier

Crown Point Retail Park

E

VICTORIA QUARTER

KING EDWARD STREET

CROWN ST

Corn Exchange

Pedestrians only

CALL LANE

BRIDGE END

SWINEGATE

SOVEREIGN STREET

MEADOW LANE

GREAT WILSON ST

NEW LANE

A639

KIDACRE STREET

HOLMES ST

M621 & M1

Varieties Theatre

ALBION PL

COMMERCIAL ST

Holy Trinity

BOAR LANE

MILL

NEW STA

Victoria Bridge

NEVILLE STREET

VICTORIA ROAD

Road Tunnel

BACK ROW

MANOR RD

INGRAM ST

BARNABAS ROAD

SWEET STREET

Schofield Shopping Centre

Bond Street Shopping Centre

Peds only STREET

LOWER

BASINGHALL ST

N

INGRAM ROW

SWEET STREET WEST

ALBION

UPPER

SINGHALL ST

PARK ROW

PARK PARADE

BEDFORD ST

GREEK ST

BOND ST

Peds only

INFIRMARY ST

CITY SQUARE

Black Prince Statue

QUEBEC ST

Leeds City Station

Road Tunnel

WATER LANE

ROAD

STREET

MARSHALL

DAVID STREET

SWEET STREET

C

PARADE

PARK CROSS STREET

PARK SQ EAST

KING STREET

YORK PLACE

Coach Station

AIRE STREET

River Aire

BATH ROAD

ROAD

PARK SQ N

PARK SQ W

Park Square

ST PAUL'S STREET

QUEEN STREET

LITTLE QUEEN ST

NORTHERN STREET

Monk Bridge

GLOBE

VIADUCT

B

Police Station

Leeds International Swimming Pool

LISBON ST

WELLINGTON STREET

Aireside Centre Retail Park

400
400
300
300
200
200
100
100
0
0
mtrs yds

Newspaper Offices

SPRINGWELL ROAD

HOLBECK LANE

WATER LANE

BRIDGE ROAD

A

MARLBOROUGH STREET

WELLINGTON RD

A65

KIRKSTALL RD

A58

Central Leeds

River Aire

Leeds & Liverpool Canal

Wellington Bridge

Emmanuel Trading Estate

SPRINGWELL ST

ILKLEY

BRADFORD & M621

2 1

LEICESTER

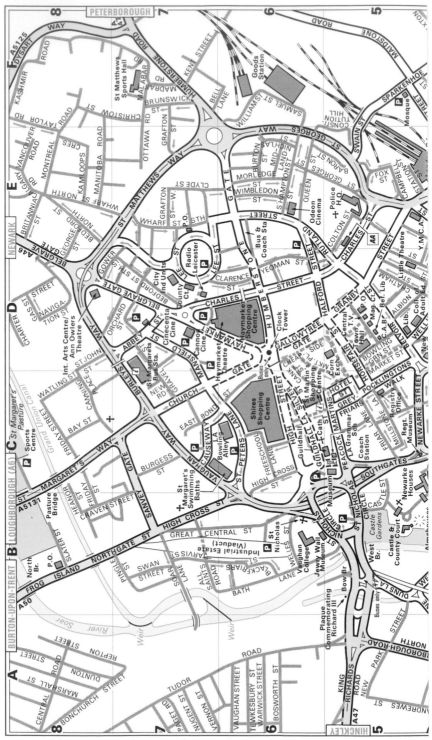

LEICESTER

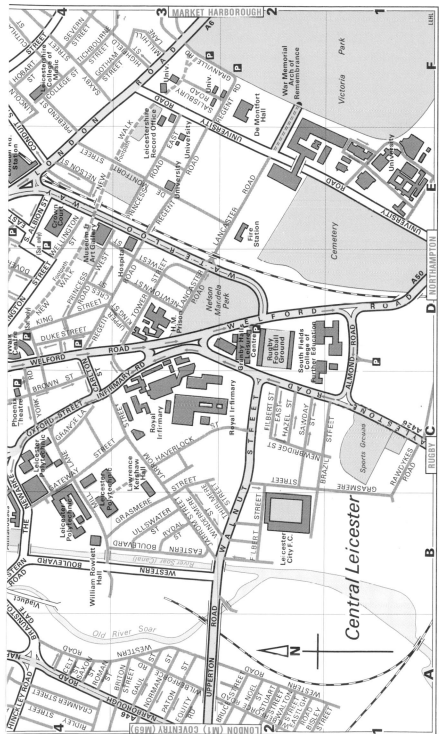

Central Leicester

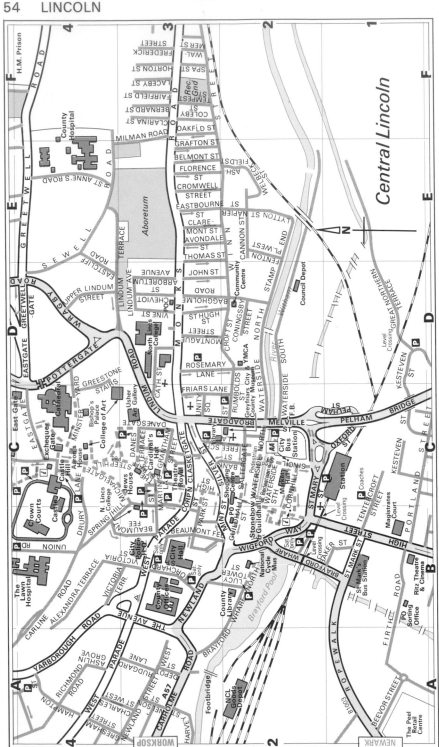

Central Lincoln

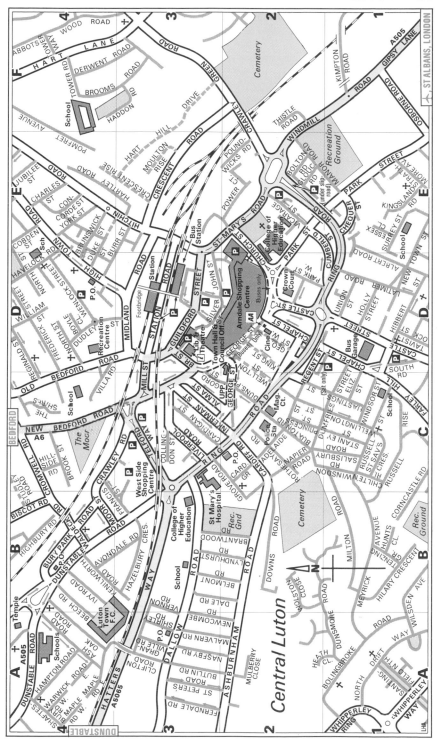

LUTON

LIVERPOOL

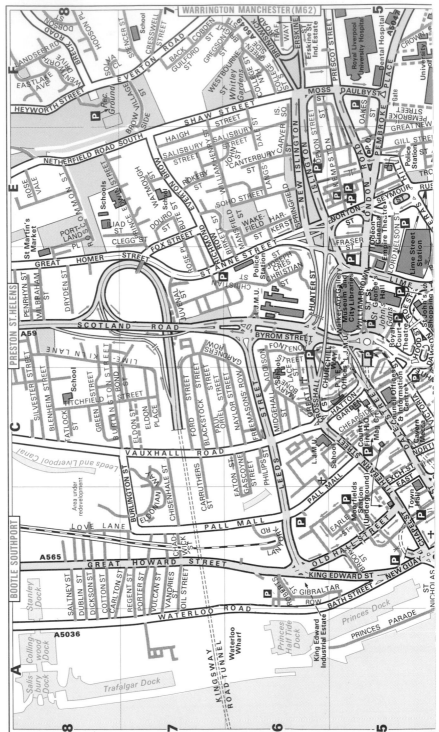

WARRINGTON MANCHESTER (M62)
A5047

School
Rec. Ground
HEYWORTH STREET
EASTLAKE AVE
LANDSEER RD
BRECK ROAD
DOBSON ST
HODSON PL
SPENCER ST
CRESSWELL ST
EVERTON ROAD
BACK GUILFORD ST
COBDEN ST
GREGSON ST
WESTBOURNE ST
WHITLEY Gardens
COLLEGE ST
A5049
BRUNSWICK WAY
TRAF WAY
Erskine St Ind. Estate
Royal Liverpool University Hospital
Dental Hospital
CROWN
Gate
PEMBROKE PLACE
GREAT NEW
GILL STREET
Police Station
RUSS
SHAW STREET
HAIGH ST
SALISBURY STREET
ROKEBY ST
SOHO STREET
CANTERBURY ST
DALE ST
CARVER SQ
LANGS
IS.
SPRINGFIELD
NEW ISLINGTON
ISLINGTON STREET
DEVON STREET
MOSS ST
OAKES
DAULBY ST
PEMBROKE STREET
SEYMOUR ST
Police Station
ROSE VALE
NETHERFIELD ROAD SOUTH
St Martin's Market
ST
PORT-LAND PL
PRINCE EDWIN STREET
ROSCOMMON ST
CLEGG ST
WATMOUGH ST
DOURO ST
BUTE ST
FOX STREET
SOHO STREET
WAKE-FIELD
HARKER ST
JOSEPH CRES
EVERTON BROW
FRASER ST
CHRISTIAN
Odeon Cinema
Empire Theatre
Lime Street Station
Schools
LIAD ST
SODA CL
BROW VILLAGE SIDE
EVERTON ROAD
WENTWORTH DRIVE
GREAT HOMER STREET
DRYDEN ST
PENRHYN ST
WILBRAHAM ST
ST ANNE STREET
ROSE PL
BIRKET ST
MANSFIELD ST
RICHMOND ROW
JUVENAL ST
Police Station
L.M.U.
HUNTER ST
BYROM STREET
St GEORGES HALL
Walker Art Gallery
Museum and City Libraries
WM BROWN
St John's Shopping
Royal Gdns
St John's Court
Lime St
WOOD ST
LORD NELSON ST
SCOTLAND ROAD
A59
PRESTON ST. HELENS
LIME-KILN LANE
SILVESTER STREET
BLENHEIM STREET
TATLOCK ST
School
FITCHFIELD STREET
GREEN ST
BURLINGTON STREET
BOND ST
ELDON ST
ELDON PLACE
FORD STREET
BLACKSTOCK ST
PAUL ST
ORIEL ST
NAYLOR STREET
FREEMASONS ROW
MIDGHALL ST
MARTY
Schools
LACE ST
ADDISON STREET
FONTENOY STREET
GARDNERS ROW
CROSSHALL
CHURCHILL
WAY
DALE
Council Offices
& Information Centre
FIRE H.Q.
Mag Court
CHEAPSIDE
HATTON GARDEN
VICTORIA ST
L.J.M.U.
School
MAG CREE
EXCH.ST
Cavern Walks
Tavern
NORTH JOHN ST
Area under redevelopment
Leeds and Liverpool Canal
VAUXHALL ROAD
BURLINGTON STREET
ELDONIAN WAY
CHISENHALE ST
CARRUTHERS ST
EATON ST
GASCOYNE ST
PHILIPS ST
PALL MALL
LEEDS ST
L.J.M.U.
GREAT CROSSHALL STREET
PALL MALL
Moorfields Station (Underground)
EARLE ST
OLD HALL STREET
TITHEBARN ST
EAST
CHAPEL ST
Town Hall
LOVE LANE
BOOTLE SOUTHPORT
A565
GREAT HOWARD STREET
STANLEY ST
SALTNEY ST
DUBLIN ST
DICKSON ST
COTTON ST
CARLTON ST
REGENT ST
PORTER ST
VULCAN ST
VANDRIES ST
CHADWICK ST
LANPORT RD
KING EDWARD ST
NEW QUAY
BATH STREET
ST NICHOLAS
WATERLOO ROAD
GIBRALTAR ROW
ROBERTS
Stanley Dock
Salis-bury Dock
Colling-wood Dock
A5036
Waterloo Wharf
King Edward Industrial Estate
Princes Half Tide Dock
Princes Dock
PRINCES PARADE
KINGSWAY ROAD TUNNEL
Trafalgar Dock

LIVERPOOL

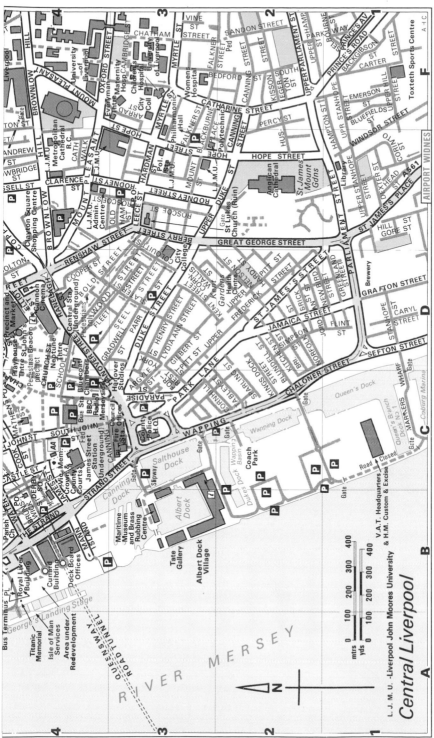

Central Liverpool

L.J.M.U. - Liverpool John Moores University

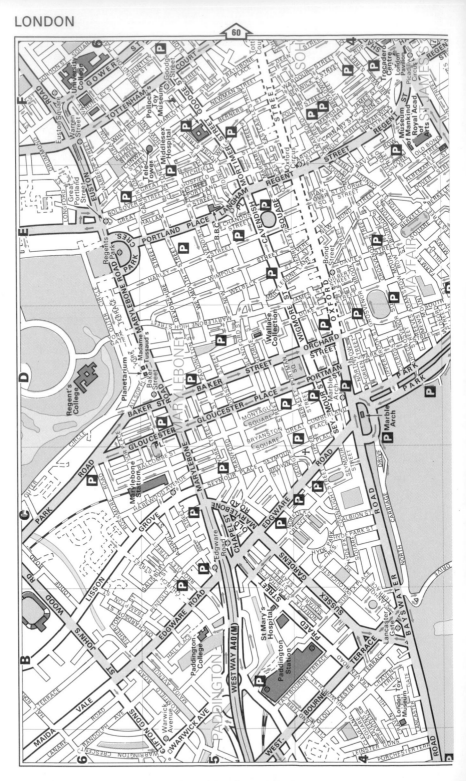

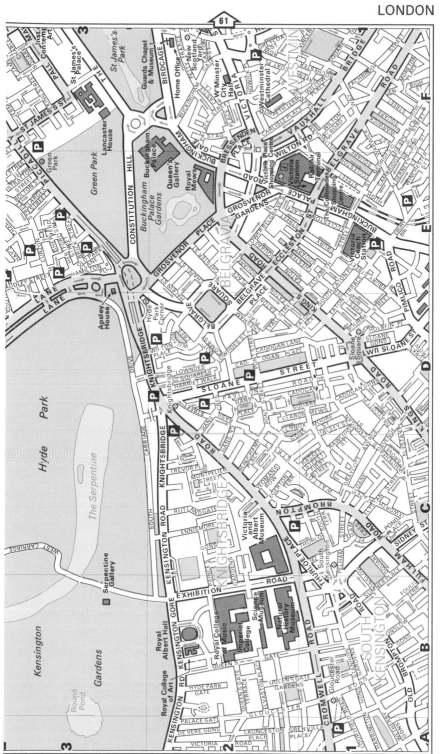

LONDON

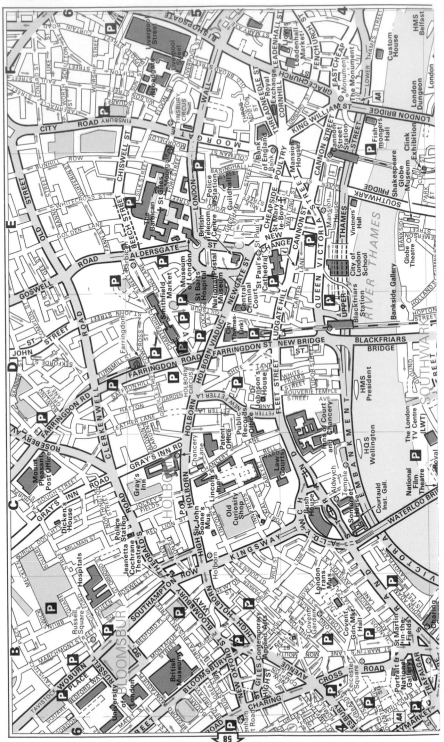

LONDON

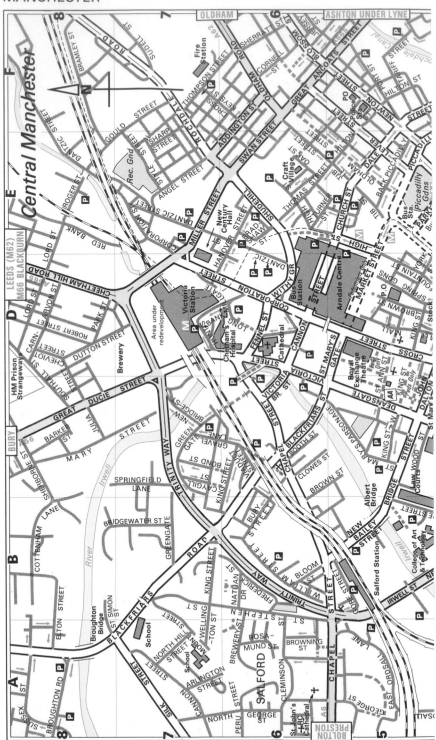

Central Manchester

MANCHESTER

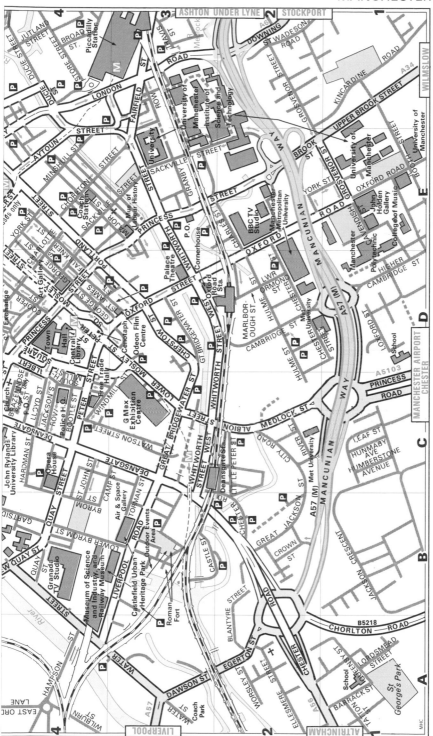

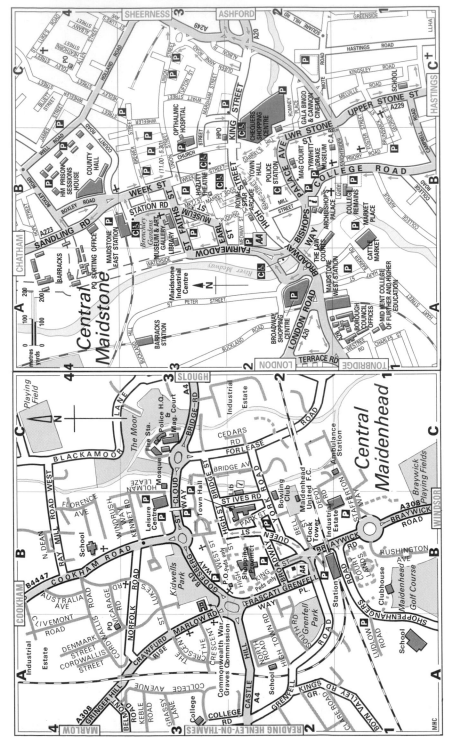

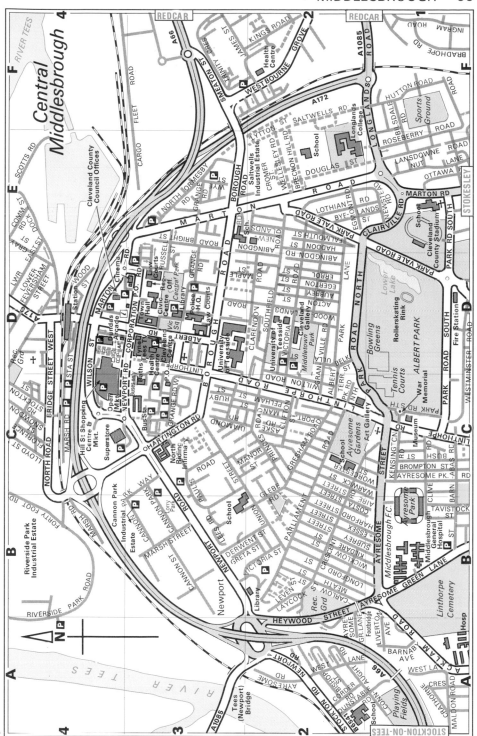

MIDDLESBROUGH

MILTON KEYNES

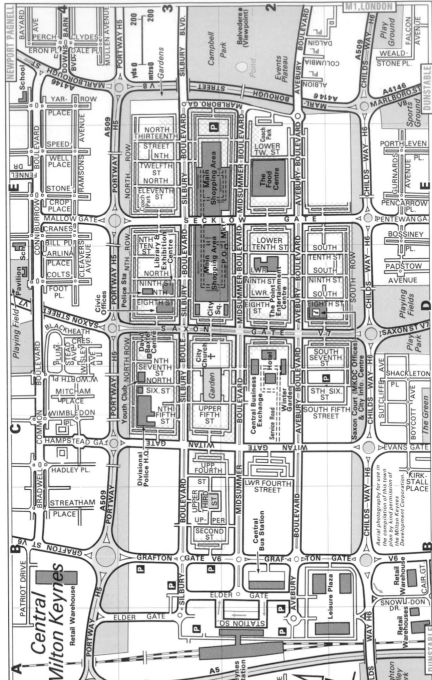

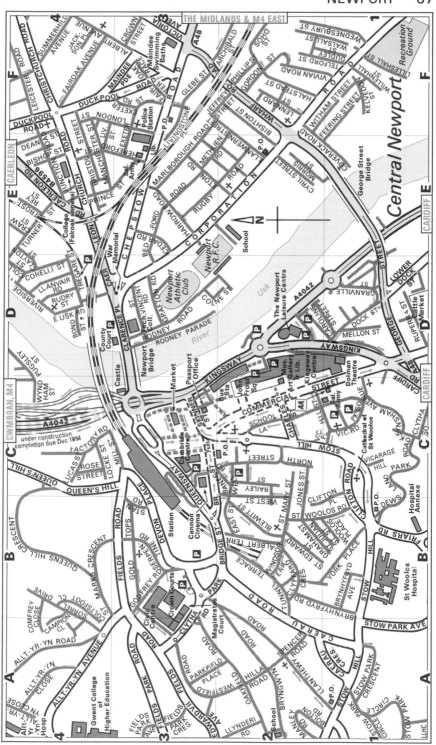

NEWPORT

Central Newport

CARDIFF

NEWCASTLE UPON TYNE

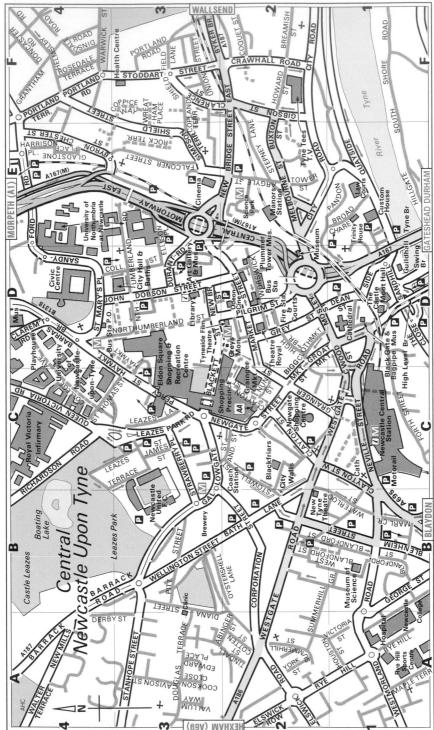

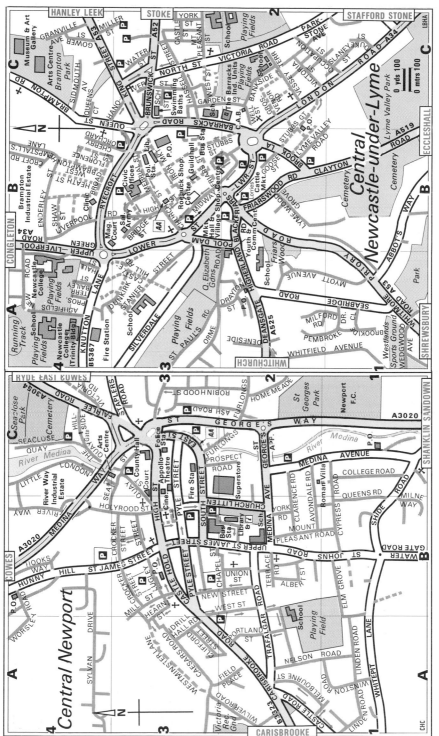

NEWPORT   NEWCASTLE UNDER LYME

Central Newcastle-under-Lyme

Central Newport

NEWBURY

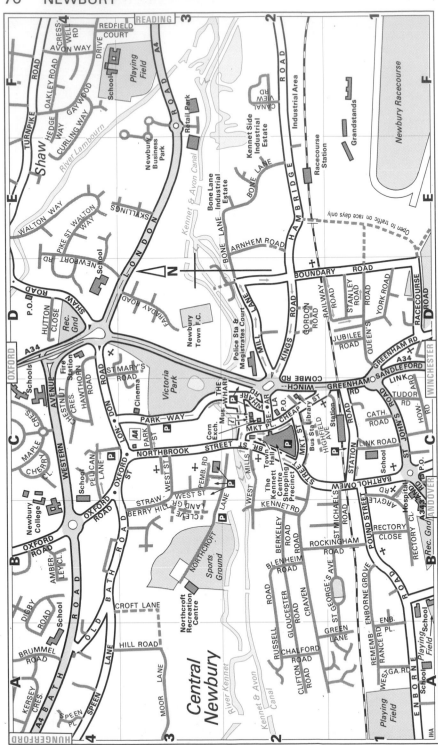

Central Newbury

NORTHAMPTON

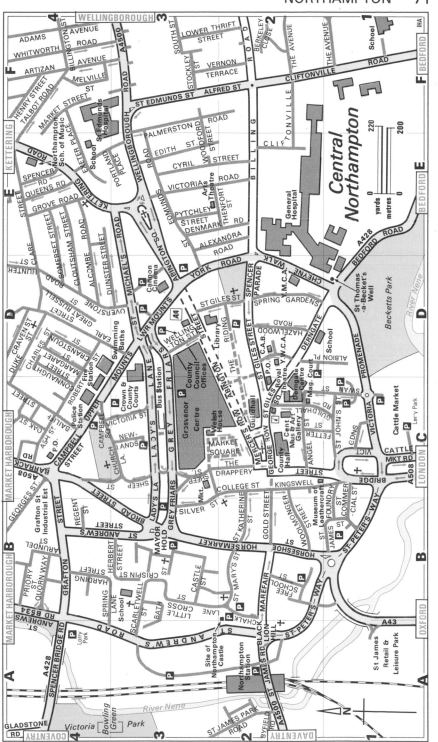

NORWICH

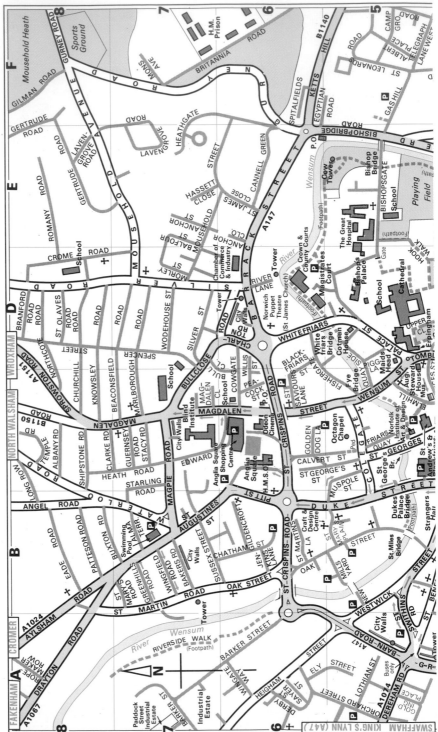

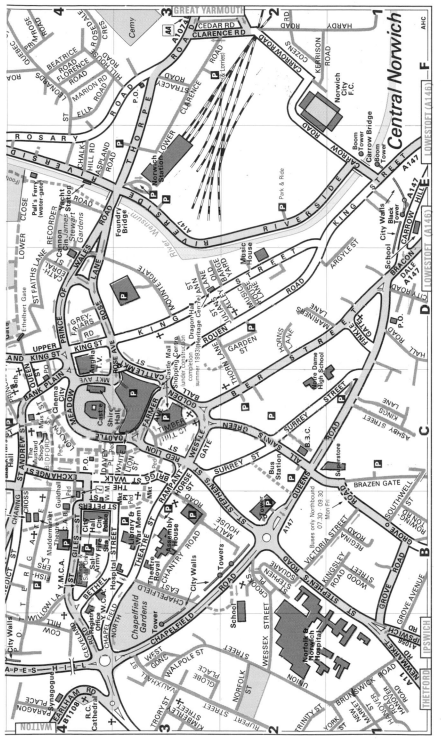

Central Norwich

NOTTINGHAM

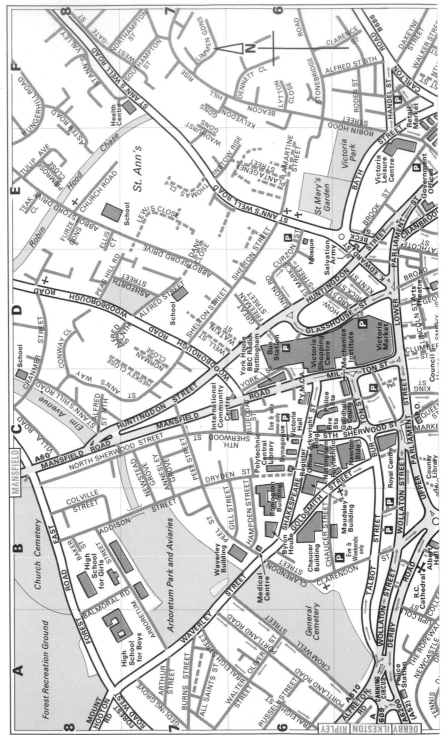

NOTTINGHAM

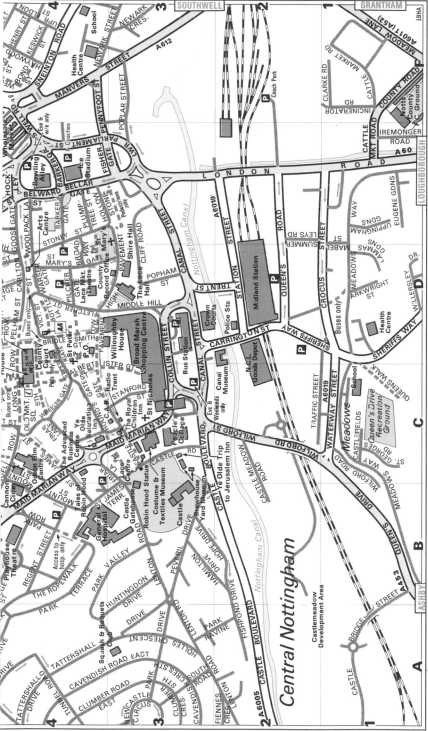

Central Nottingham

OXFORD

Central Oxford

LONDON (A40)

N

University Parks

yds 0   100   200   300   400
mtrs 0   100   200   300   400

FERRY ROAD

Holywell

...erwell

Mill Stream

Merton College Playing Fields

St Catherine's College

MANOR

Inst of Statistics
Law & English Library

Cemetery

Magdalen Grove (Deer Park)

Magdalen College

Magdalen Bridge

The Plain

University Private Botanic Gardens

ROSE LANE

HIGH STREET

Merton Field

Playing Fields

LONGWALL ST

Linacre College

New College Sports Ground

Merton College Sports Ground

Balliol College Sports Ground

JOWETT WALK

MANSFIELD ROAD

SAVILLE ROAD

HOLYWELL STREET

New College

St Edmund's Hall

Queen's College

University College

MERTON STREET

Merton College

Oriel College

Corpus Christi College

Christ Church

University Science Area

University Museum

SOUTH PARKS ROAD

South Mansfield College

Manchester College

Rhodes House

Wadham College

Indian Institute

Sheldonian Theatre

History of Science Museum

Clarendon

Hertford College

All Souls College

Radcliffe Camera

St Mary's Church

PARKS ROAD

New Bodleian Library

BROAD STREET

Trinity College

Balliol College

Old Ashmolean

Bodleian Library

Exeter College

Trinity Coll

Lincoln Coll

Brasenose College

All Saints Church

TURL ST

Jesus College

MARKET STREET

City Mkt.

BEAR LA

HIGH STREET

AA

Town Hall

Oxford Blue

Museum of Modern Art

Clarendon

ST ALDATES

Pembroke College

KEBLE ROAD

Keble College

BLACK HALL ROAD

MUSEUM ROAD

PARKS ROAD

St John's College

MAGDALEN STREET

ST GILES STREET

CORNMARKET STREET

ST MICHAEL

QUEEN STREET

St St Buses Only

NEW INN HALL

Carfax

Clarendon Shopping Centre

Westgate Shopping Centre

STEBBE'S ST

BANBURY ROAD

St Anne's College

Green College

Observatory

Acland Hosp

Radcliffe Infirmary

Somerville

Regents Park College

WELLINGTON SQ

St Cross Coll

Pusey Ho.

St John's Pusey St

Ashmolean Mus.

Cannon Cinema

Apollo Theatre

GLOUC ST

Cine

St Peter's College

NEW ROAD

County Hall

Oxford Castle

H M Prison

PARADISE ST

PARADISE SQUARE

CASTLE

WOODSTOCK ROAD

P.O.

CLARENDON ST

ST JOHN ST

BEAUMONT STREET

WORCESTER ST

GEORGE STREET

Cannon Mkt.

Bus Sta

Nuffield College

Fire Station

HYTHE BRIDGE STREET

St THOMAS STREET

MARSH LA

TID.

ADELAIDE STREET

OBSERVATORY ST

WALTON STREET

Eye Hospital

University Press

School

Phoenix Cinema

JERICHO ST

JUXON STREET

CRANHAM ST

VICTOR ST

HART ST

ALBERT ST

CLARENDON ST

GREAT CLARENDON ST

CARDIGAN ST

NELSON ST

WALTON CRES

RICHMOND RD

WORC PL

Synagogue

Ruskin College

Worcester College

Cricket Ground

Castle Mill Stream

College of Further Education

HOLLYBUSH ROW

St THOMAS STREET

OSNEY LANE

OSNEY LANE

Oxford Business Centre

REWLEY ROAD

PARK END STREET

Station

BECKET STREET

CRIPLEY ROAD

MILL STREET

ARTHUR STREET

Oxford Canal

CANAL

Cemetery

Castle Mill Stream

Sheep-wash Channel

River Thames

ABBEY ROAD

A420

SWINDON

BATH STREET

BOULTER STREET

JEUNE ST

A420

ST CLEMENTS

Angel Meadow

CALEFAX

yds 0

mtrs 0

PETERBOROUGH

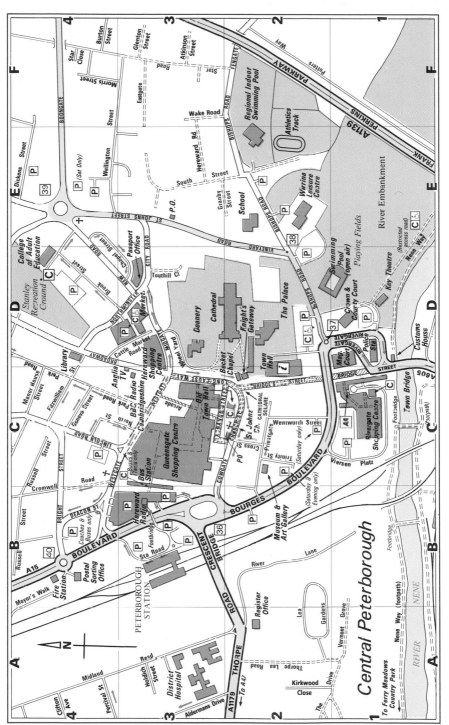

Central Peterborough

PLYMOUTH

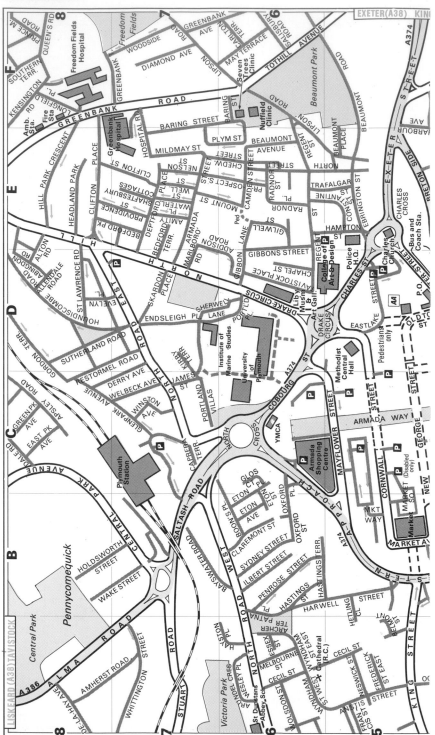

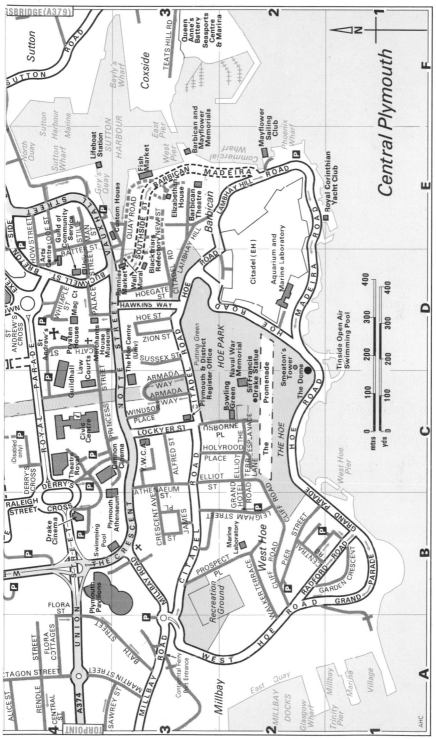

PLYMOUTH

Central Plymouth

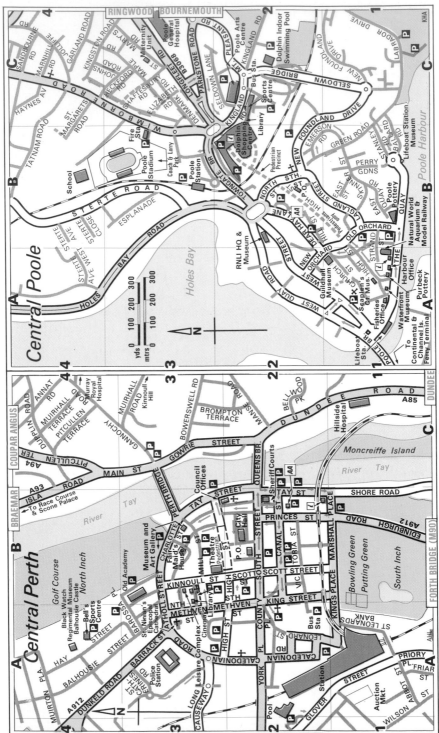

Central Poole

RINGWOOD BOURNEMOUTH

Poole General Hospital
Maternity Unit
Poole Arts Centre
Dolphin Indoor Swimming Pool
SELDOWN BRIDGE
NEW FOUNDLAND DRIVE
LABRADOR DRIVE
KHA
Sports Centre
Library
Bus Sta.
Dolphin Shopping Centre
Pedestrian Precinct
EMERSON RD
GREEN ROAD
PERRY GDNS
Lifeboat Station
Poole Harbour
Fire Sta.
Coach & Lorry Park
Poole Stadium
Poole Station
STANLEY RD
BALLARD RD
EAST QUAY
EAST ST
TWINE RD
Poole Pottery
Natural World Aquarium & Model Railway
School
STERTE ROAD
ESPLANADE
HOLES BAY ROAD
Holes Bay
RNLI HQ & Museum
WEST QUAY ROAD
NEW ORCHARD
WEST ORCHARD
Guildhall Museum
CHURCH ST
HIGH ST
OLD ORCHARD
STRAND ST
THE QUAY
Scaplen's Crt. Mus.
Fisheries Museum
Waterfront Museum
Harbour Office
Purbeck Pottery
To Continental & Channel Is. Ferry Terminal
Lifeboat Sta.
POOLE BR.
yds 0 100 200 300
mtrs 0 100 200 300
N

Central Perth

DUNDEE
COUPAR ANGUS
ANNAT RD
DUPLIN RD
MUIRHALL RD
MURRAY ROYAL HOSPITAL
Kinnoull Hill
MUIRHALL TERRACE
PITCULLEN TERRACE
GANNOCHY RD
BOWERSWELL RD
MANSE ROAD
BROMPTON TERRACE
BELLWOOD PK
DUNDEE ROAD
A85
Hillside Hospital
Moncreiffe Island
River Tay
C
BRAEMAR
A94
A93
ISLA ROAD
MAIN ST
GOWRIE STREET
To Race Course & Scone Palace
PERTH BRIDGE
TAY ST
CHARLOTTE ST
Council Offices
Sheriff Courts
QUEENS BR.
AA
River Tay
SHORE ROAD
Golf Course
Black Watch Regimental Museum
Balhousie Castle
Bell's Sports Centre
North Inch
Museum and Art Gallery
Maid's House
Theatre
CITY HALL
MILL ST
HIGH ST
SOUTH ST
PRINCES STREET
CANAL ST
VICTORIA ST
MARSHALL PLACE
KINGS PLACE
EDINBURGH ROAD
A912
FORTH BRIDGE (M90)
St Ninian's Episcopal Cathedral
Old Academy
Cinema
Library
Pedestrian
P.O.
SCOTT ST
METHVEN ST
KING STREET
Bus Sta
Bowling Green
Putting Green
South Inch
ST LEONARD'S BANK
HAY STREET
BALHOUSIE STREET
BARROSSA ST
ATHOLL STREET
BARRACK ST
ST PAUL'S CALEDONIAN RD
Police Station
COUNTY PL
YORK PL
CALEDONIAN RD
LEONARD ST
Station
Pool
GLOVER STREET
PRIORY PL
FRIAR ST
Auction Mkt.
WILSON ST
ABBOT ST
MURTON PL
A912
DUNKELD ROAD
CAUSEWAY
LONG LEISURE COMPLEX
N

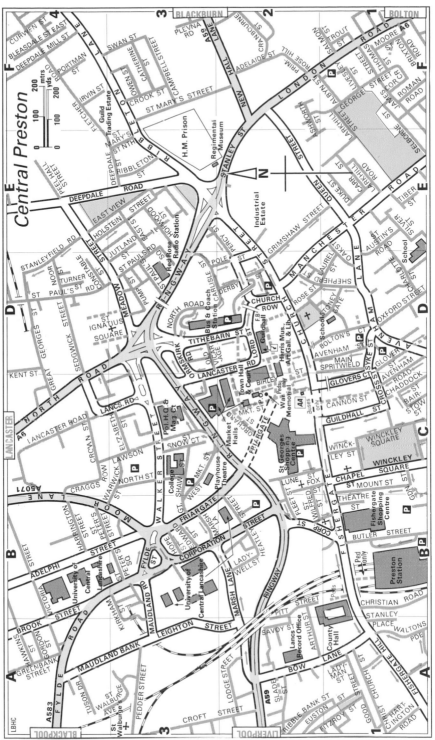

PRESTON

Central Preston

PORTSMOUTH

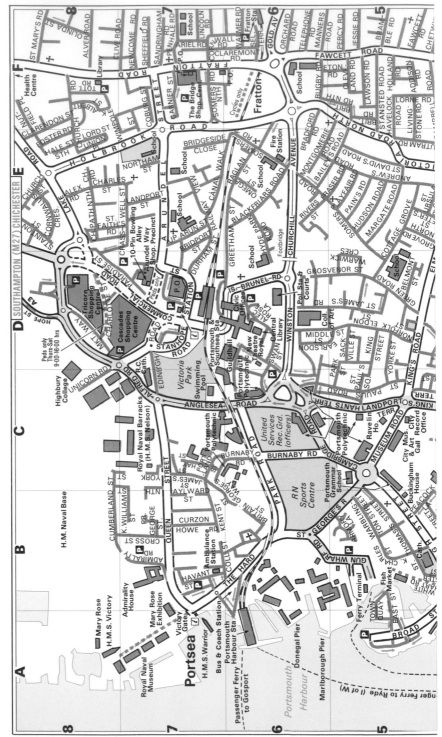

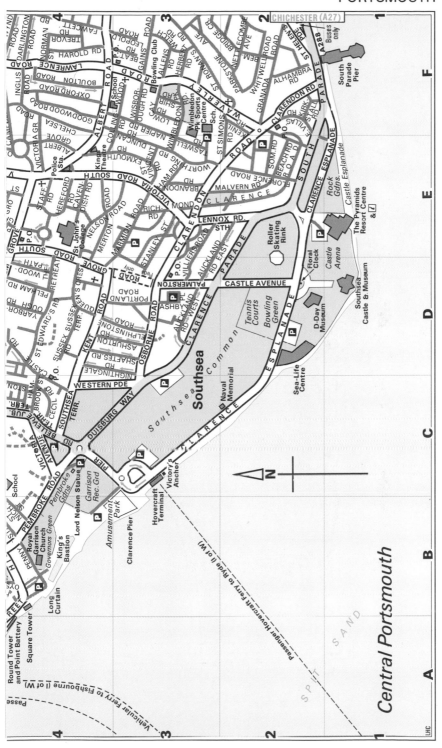

PORTSMOUTH

Central Portsmouth

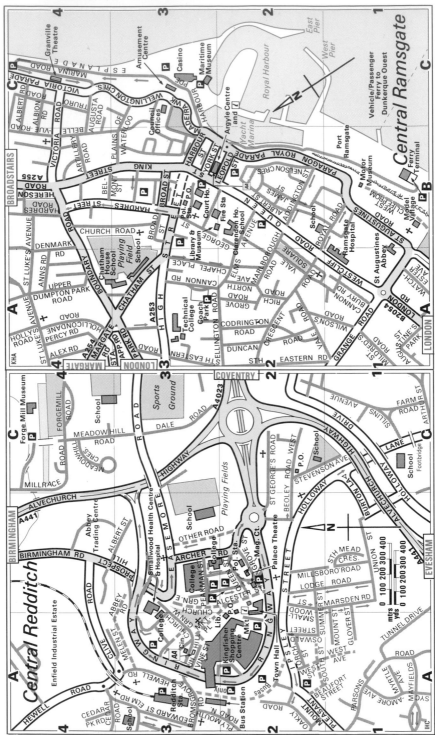

RAMSGATE

REDDITCH

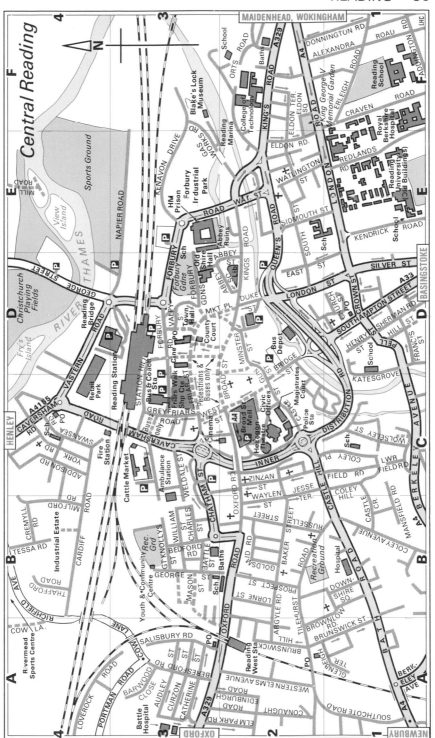

READING

Central Reading

REIGATE

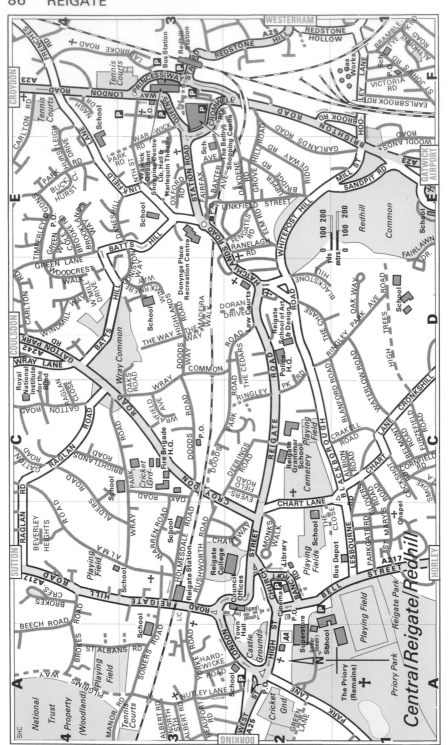

RUGBY   RIPON

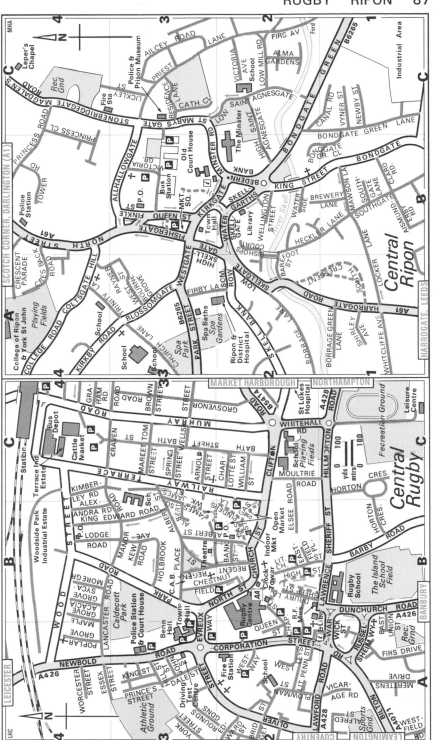

Ripon (map labels)

MHA
Leper's Chapel
Police & Prison Museum
AILCEY ROAD
LANE
PRIEST LANE
FIRS AV
LOW MILL RD
ALMA GARDENS
VICTORIA AVE
School
Rec Gnd
Fire Sta
LICKLEY ST
RESIDENCE
ST MARY'S GATE
MINSTER RD
LOW SAINT AGNESGATE
CATH. CL.
B6265
Industrial Area
STONEBRIDGEGATE
MAGDALENS ROAD
PRINCESS CL.
PRINCESS RD
TOWER
Old Court House
The Minster
HIGH SAINT AGNESGATE
BONDGATE GREEN LANE
CANAL RD
VYNER ST
NEWBY ST
BONDGATE
ALLHALLOWGATE
VICTORIA GR.
P.O.
Bus Station
MKT. SQ.
KIRKGATE
BANK
BEDERN
KING STREET
BONDGATE GR. CL.
SOUTHGATE LANE
MAWSON LA
CLARO RD.
Police Station
NORTH STREET
FINKLE ST
QUEEN ST
Twn Hall
SKELL GARTHS
Library
WELLINGTON STREET
River Skell
BREWERY
SIDE
SOUTH LANE
ASMUND ERD
CRESCENT PARADE
CRES BACK
FISHERGATE
WESTGATE
HIGH SKELLGATE
WATER SKELL ST
BISHOPS COURT
HECKLER LANE
BAREFOOT ST
LOCKER
College of Ripon & York St John
KIRKBY ROAD
COLLEGE ROAD
COLTSGATE HILL
RAYNER ST
WEST ST
BLOSSOMGATE
TRINITY LANE
School
FIRBY LA.
SCM ROW
LOW SKELLGATE
HARROGATE ROAD
BORRAGE GREEN LANE
SHIRLEY AVE
WHITCLIFFE AVE
Playing Fields
CHURCH LANE
B6265
PARK STREET
School
Spa Park
Spa Baths
Spa Gardens
Ripon & District Hospital
SKELL BANK
LANE
BORRAGE LANE
Central Ripon
HARROGATE, LEEDS
A61
SCOTCH CORNER DARLINGTON (A1)

Rugby (map labels)

LHC
Station
Woodside Park Industrial Estate
Terrace Ind Estate
Bus Depot
Cattle Market
GRAHAM RD
CRAVEN ST
BROWN ROAD
GROSVENOR ROAD
MARKET HARBOROUGH   NORTHAMPTON
St Lukes Hospital
A428
Leisure Centre
WOOD STREET
LANCASTER ROAD
CALDECOTT PARK
MOREGROVE
SYCAMORE GROVE
ACACIA GROVE
MAPLE GROVE
POPLAR GROVE
KIMBERLEY RD
ALEXANDRA RD
KING EDWARD ROAD
MANOR ROAD
KEW ROAD
HOLBROOK
P.O.
LODGE ROAD
TOM STREET
MARKET STREET
SPRING STREET
WELLS STREET
ARNOLD STREET
CHARLOTTE ST
WILLIAM STREET
BATH STREET
RAILWAY TERRACE
ST JAMES
JAMES WK
ALBERT RD
ALBERT ST
C.A.B.
REGENT ST
CHESTNUT FIELD
PLACE
WHITEHALL RD
CLIFTON RD
MOULTRIE ROAD
HILLMORTON ROAD
School Playing Fields
HORTON CRES.
HORTON CRES.
Recreation Ground
Central Rugby
yds 0 100
mtrs 0 100
ELSEE ROAD
Open Market
Indoor Mkt
Theatre
BANK ST
CHURCH ST
NORTH ST
Clock Tower
Town Hall
Rugby Centre
Rugby School
Benn Hall
Police Station & Court House
EVREUX WAY
ST WAY
DRURY LA.
HIGH ST
CHAPEL ST
SHEEP ST
LIT. CHURCH ST
LIT. PENNINGTON ST
SHERIFF ST
BARBY ROAD
LAWRENCE SHERIFF ST
EAST ST
EAST UNION ST
The Island School Field
DUNCHURCH ROAD
A426
BANBURY
Rec Gnd
WICK ST
QUEEN ST
R.F.
LIBRARY
WAR MEM.
RUSSELL
SHEEP WAY
FIRS DRIVE
VICARAGE RD
MERTTENS DRIVE
WEST FIELD
A4071 WEST FIELD RD
BILTON RD
Sports Gnd.
OLIVER ST
BRIDGET ST
LAWFORD RD
A428
PLOWMAN ST
WARD ST
WINFRED ST
GAS ST
DALE ST
HILL ST
STATION ROAD
NEWBOLD ROAD
A426
WORCESTER STREET
ESSEX STREET
KING ST
PRINCE'S STREET
CORPORATION STREET
Fire Station
Driving Test Centre
School
WEST WAY
Athletic Ground
YORK STREET
GROUNDS GDNS
LEICESTER
COVENTRY
LEAMINGTON
Central Rugby

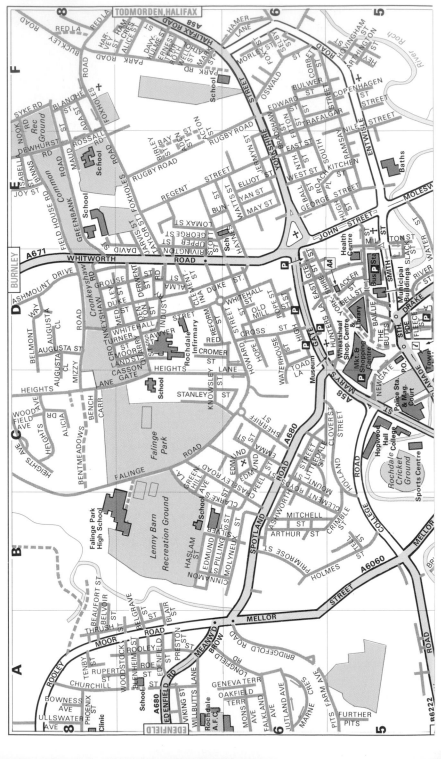

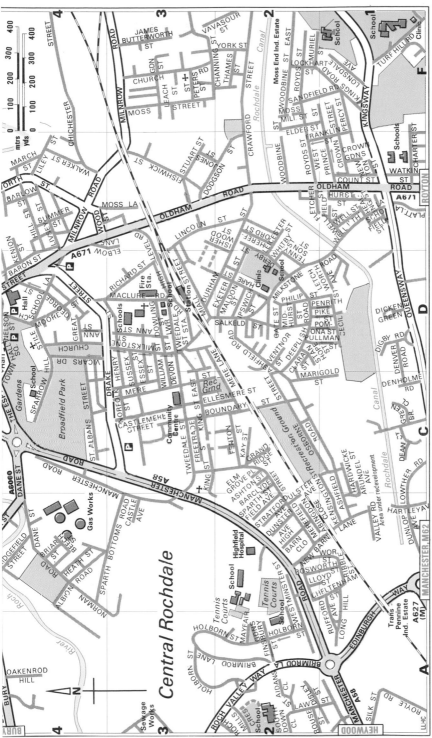

ROCHDALE

ST ANDREWS

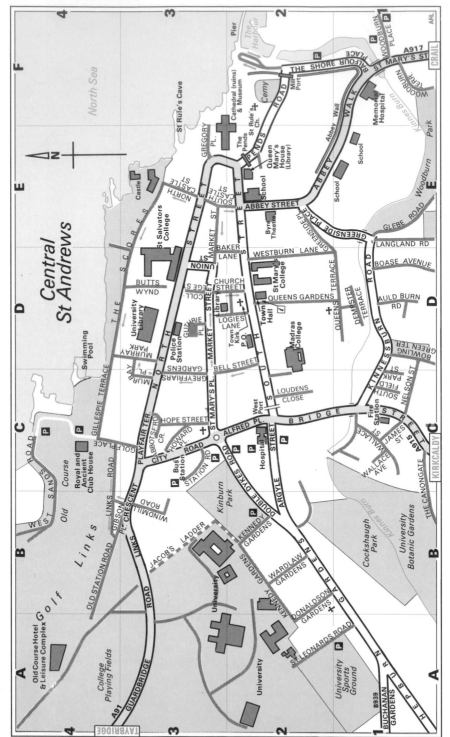

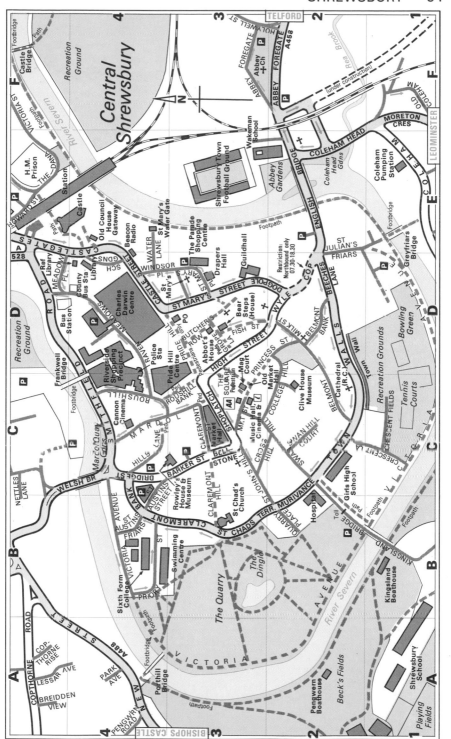

SHREWSBURY

SALISBURY

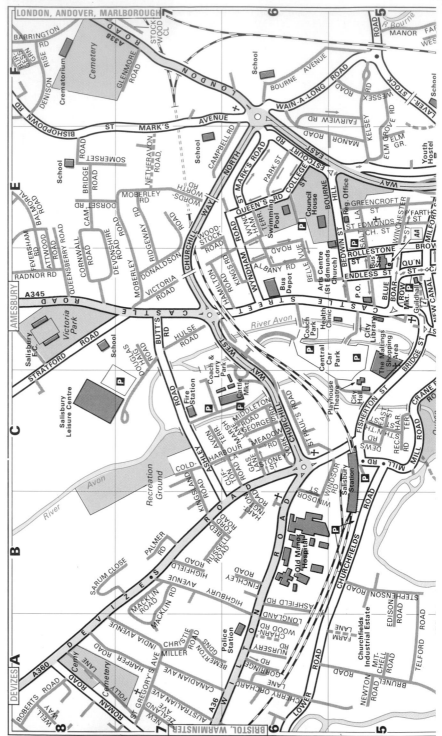

SALISBURY

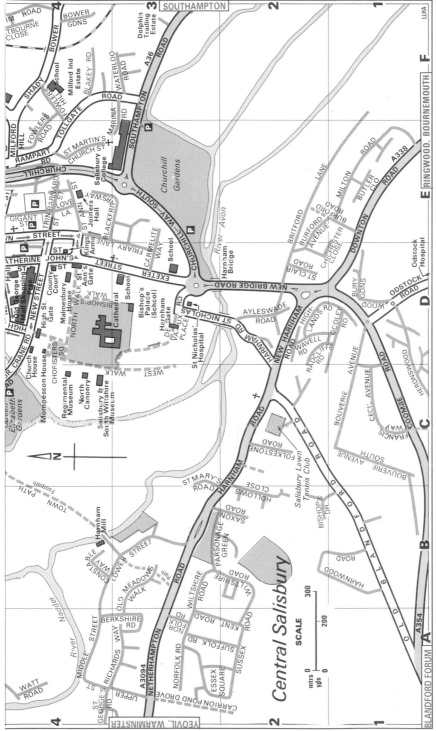

Central Salisbury

SCALE

mtrs 0   200   300
yds 0

SHEFFIELD

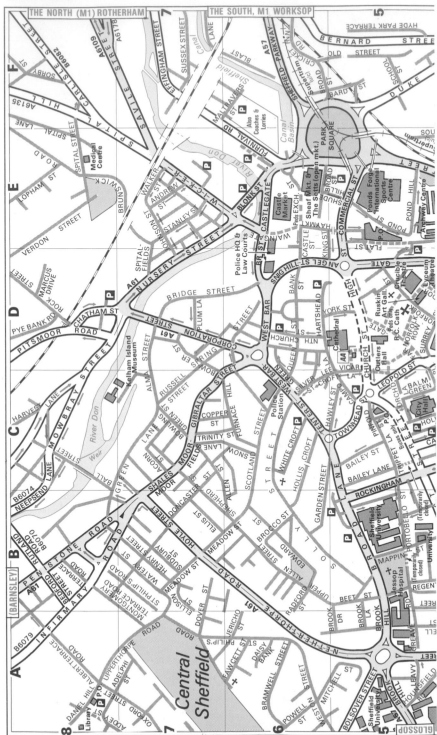

THE NORTH (M1) ROTHERHAM

THE SOUTH, M1 WORKSOP

Central Sheffield

[BARNSLEY]

GLOSSOP

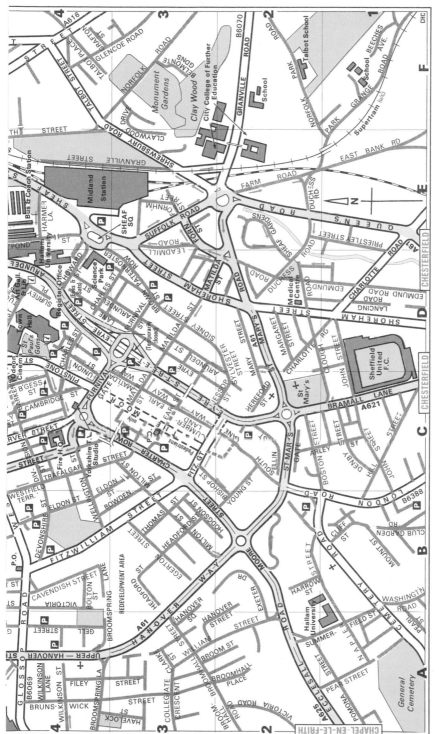

SHEFFIELD

SLOUGH

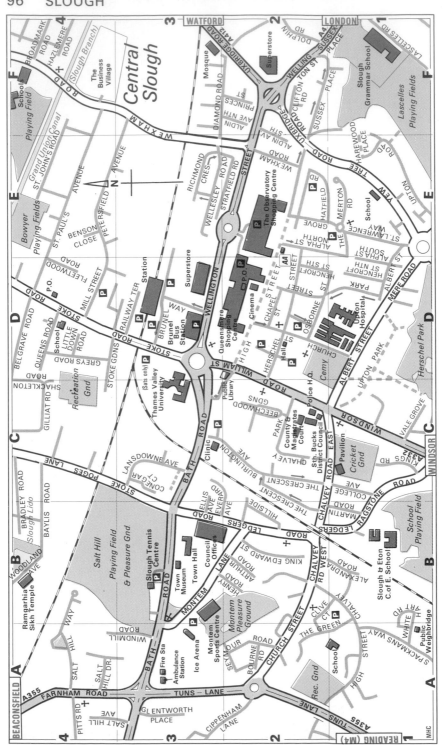

Central Slough

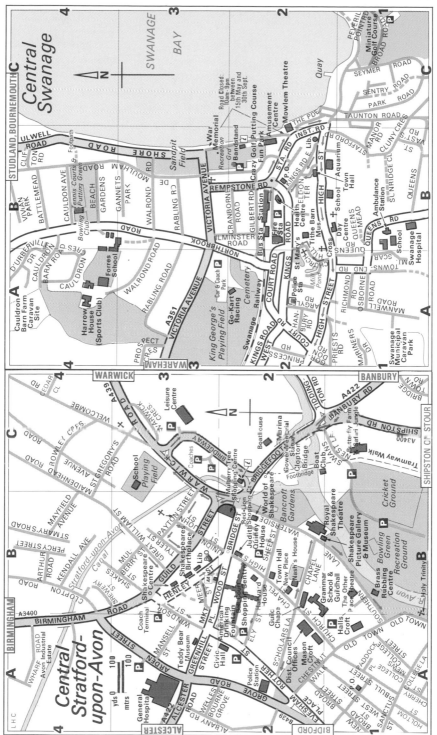

STRATFORD SWANAGE

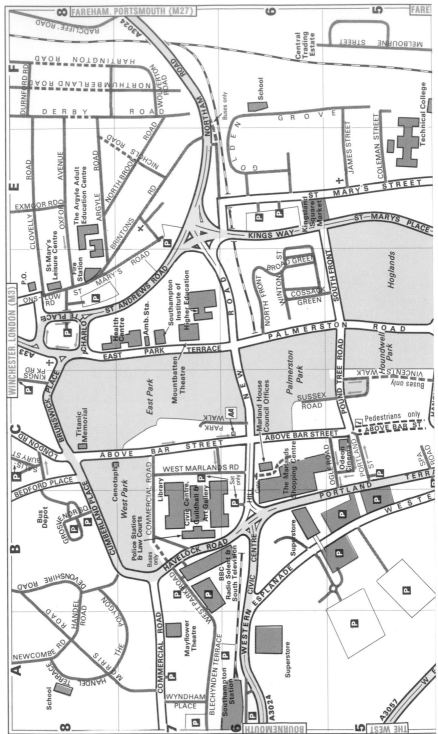

SOUTHAMPTON

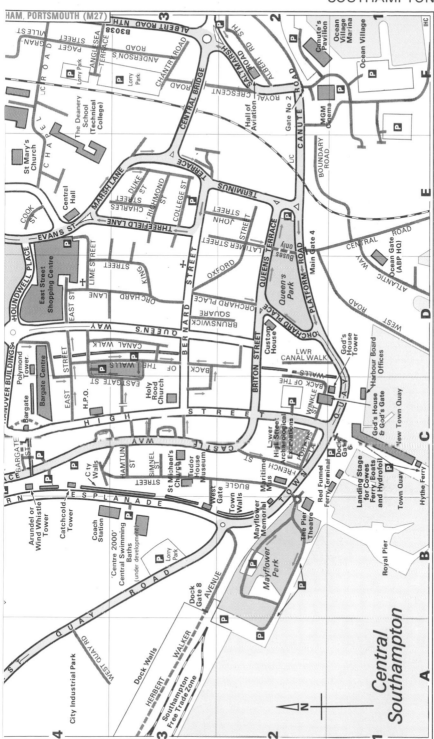

Central Southampton

N

SUNDERLAND

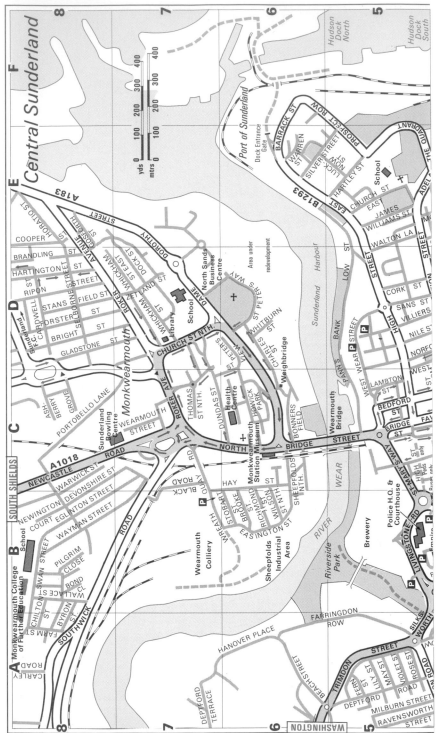

Central Sunderland

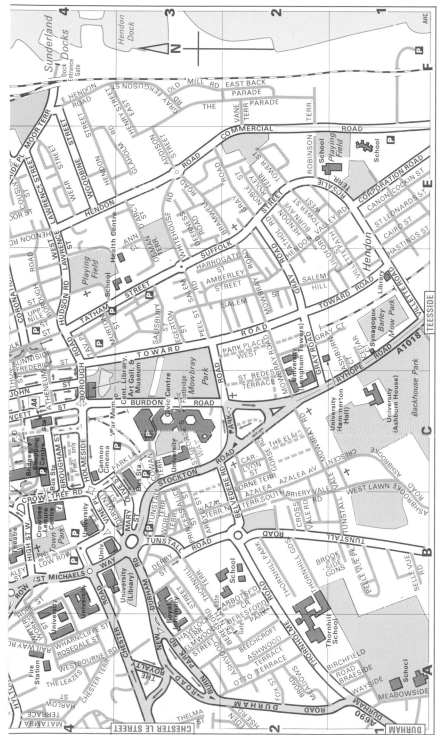

SUNDERLAND

SWANSEA

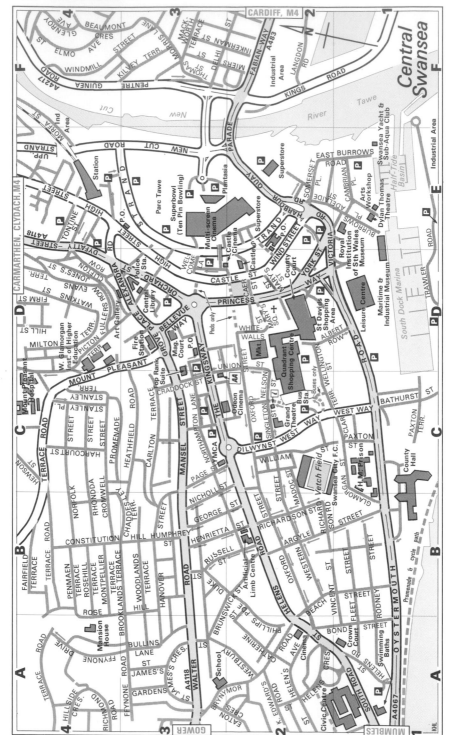

Central Swansea

CARDIFF, M4

CARMARTHEN, CLYDACH, M4

GOWER

MUMBLES

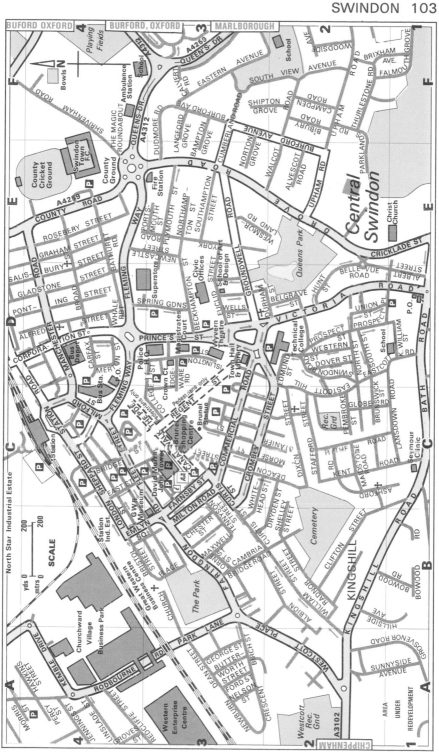

SWINDON

WARWICK WINDSOR

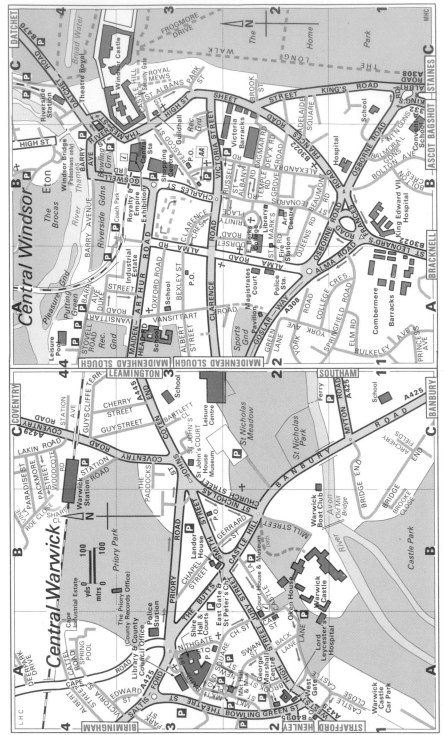

Central Windsor

DATCHET
DATCHET ROAD B470
Broad Water
Windsor Castle
Theatre Royal
Riverside Station
HIGH ST
Eton
The Brocas
River Thames
Windsor Bridge (Pedestrians only)
Barry Avenue
Riverside Gdns
Coach Park
The Pleasure Gnd
Putting Green
BARRY AVE
DUKE STREET
STOVELL ROAD
Rec. Gnd
Leisure Pool
MAIDENHEAD SLOUGH

ROYAL MEWS
CASTLE HILL
ST ALBANS
Security Gate
Guildhall
Rec. Grd
HIGH ST
THAMES ST
PEASCOD ST
Central Sta
Shopping Centre
Bowling Grn
GOSWELL RD
CHARLES ST
ARTHUR ROAD
OXFORD ROAD
Industrial Estate
Royalty & Empire Exhibition
CLARENCE CRES
ALMA RD
BEXLEY ST
P.O.
School
VANSITTART
MAIDENHEAD RD
School
VANSITTART ROAD
ALBERT STREET
CLARENCE ROAD

SHEET STREET
BROOK
KING'S ROAD
VICTORIA STREET
Victoria Barracks
RUSSELL ST
ALBANY RD
BAGMAR RD
GROVE RD
DEVX RD
TEMPLE RD
LEONARDS
ST MARK'S
Library E Berks College
DORSET RD
ST LEONARD'S ROAD
Fire Stn
QUEENS RD
Police Sta.
Magistrates Court
Pavilion
Sports Gnd
GOSLAR WAY
GREEN LANE
A308
YORK AVE
TRINITY PLACE
Art Centre
BEAUMONT RD
ALMA ROAD
COLLEGE CRES
YORK ROAD
SPRINGFIELD ROAD
ELM RD
BULKELEY AVE
PRINCESS AVE

STREET
FRANCES RD
ADELAIDE SQUARE
B3022
Hospital
ALEXANDRA ROAD
OSBORNE ROAD
FRANCES ROAD
ST LEONARD'S ROAD
Combermere Barracks
Barracks
KING'S ROAD
ALBERT ROAD A308
STAINES
School
FNTN GDNS
BALMORAL GDNS
BOLTON AVE
BOLTON CRES
King Edward VII Hospital
Convent School
B302?
ASCOT BAGSHOT
BRACKNELL
Long Walk
The Home Park
FROGMORE DRIVE
N
MHC

Central Warwick

COVENTRY
COVENTRY ROAD A429
STATION AVE
GUYSCLIFFE TERR
LAKIN ROAD
VIA PARADISE ST
PACKMORE STREET
WOODCOTE RD
ROE CLOSE
SHARPE CL
CAPE ROAD
Cape Industrial Estate
The Priory (County Records Office)
CATTEL ROAD
SPRING POOL
DEER PARK DRIVE
Library & County Council Office
NORTHGATE ST
VICTORIA STREET
ALBERT STREET
EDWARD ST
CAPE ROAD A425
SALTISFORD
PARK ST
BIRMINGHAM
LHC

CHERRY STREET
GUY STREET
COTEN END
A445
School
BARTLETT CL
St John's COURT
St John's House Museum
Leisure Centre
Warwick STATION
Station Road
THE PADDOCKS
N
Priory Park
100 yds 0   100 mtrs 0
The Priory
Police Station
PRIORY ROAD
SMITH STREET
THE BUTTS
Chapel STREET
Landor House
ST NICHOLAS CHURCH STREET
St Nicholas Church
P.O.
GERRARD ST
CASTLE HILL
Court House & Museum
Shire Hall & Courts
East Gate & St Peter's Ch.
CASTLE ST
Oken House
Warwick Castle
MILL STREET
BACK LANE
CASTLE LANE
CASTLE CLOSE
NEW ST
George STREET
Court House
Marshalls Centre
SWAN ST
MKT
Mkt Hall & Mus
Lord Leycester's Hospital
West Gate
HIGH ST
BOWLING GREEN ST
THEATRE ST
BROOK ST
MKT SQUARE
OLD SQUARE
JURY STREET
STRATFORD HENLEY
WEST ST
CASTLE ST A429
Warwick Castle Car Park

LEAMINGTON
SOUTHAM
St Nicholas Meadow
St Nicholas Park
Ferry
MYTON ROAD A425
BANBURY ROAD
BRIDGE END
BROOKE CLOSE
ARCHERY FIELDS
BRIDGE END
A425
School
BANBURY
Warwick Boat Club
Old Mill Bridge
River Avon
Castle Park
Warwick Castle
COVENTRY ROAD

WEYMOUTH

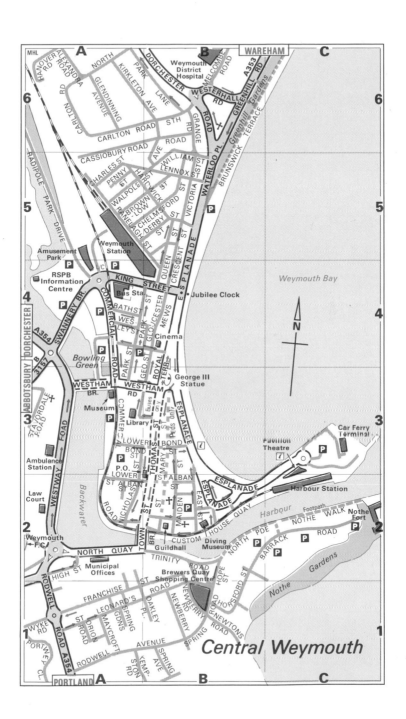

MHL

A B WAREHAM C

NORTH
KIRKLETON AVE
PARK
DORCHESTER LANE
Weymouth
District
Hospital
WESTERHALL RD
MELCOMBE RD
GREENHILL RD
A353

6 6

HANOVER RD
ALEXANDRA ROAD
GLENDINNING AVENUE
CARLTON RD
GRANGE RD
STH
Greenhill Gardens
BRUNSWICK TERRACE
WATERLOO PL.

CARLTON ROAD STH ROAD

CASSIOBURY ROAD
CHARLES ST
PENNY ST
AVE
WILLIAM ST
LENNOX ST
VICTORIA ST

5
RADIPOLE PARK DRIVE
WALPOLE ST
HARDWICK ST
BROWN LOW ST
RANELAGH ST
CHELMSFORD ST
DERBY ST
QUEEN ST
CRESCENT ST
E. ESPLANADE

5

Weymouth
Station
Amusement
Park
RSPB
Information
Centre
P
I/C
P
Bus Sta.
KING STREET
Jubilee Clock
Weymouth Bay

4
DORCHESTER
A354
B3157
SWANNERY BR.
COMMERCIAL
BATH ST
WES
LEYS
PARK ST
GLOUCESTER ST
GEO. ST
MEWS
ROYAL TERR.
Cinema
N

4

Bowling
Green
WESTHAM BR.
WESTHAM RD
Museum
P
COMMERCIAL ROAD
George III
Statue

3
ABBOTSBURY
STAVORDALE ROAD
Library
LOWER BOND ST
BOND ST
ST THOMAS ST
ST MARY ST
ST ALBAN ST
ESPLANADE
i
Pavilion
Theatre
i
Car Ferry
Terminal
P

3

Ambulance
Station
P.O.
LOWER
ST ALBAN ST
Peds only
EAST ST
Harbour Station
P

Law
Court
WESTWAY ROAD
Backwater
NICHOLAS ST
TOWN BR.
MAIDEN ST
ESPLANADE
P
Harbour
Footpath
NOTHE WALK
Nothe
Fort
P

2
Weymouth
F.C.
NORTH QUAY
CUSTOM HOUSE QUAY
Diving
Museum
NORTH PDE
BARRACK RD
NOTHE ROAD
P

2

HIGH ST
Municipal
Offices
TRINITY ROAD
Guildhall
HOPE ST
HORSFORD ST
Nothe Gardens

RODWELL ROAD A354
FRANCHISE
LEONARD'S RD
Brewers Quay
Shopping Centre
NEWBERRY ROAD
NEWTONS ROAD

1
WYKE RD
PORTWEY CL.
SPRING GDNS
OAKLEY PL.
ORION ROAD
MAYCROFT RD
RODWELL AVENUE
KEMPSTON RD
SPRING RD
Central Weymouth

1

PORTLAND A B C

WEMBLEY

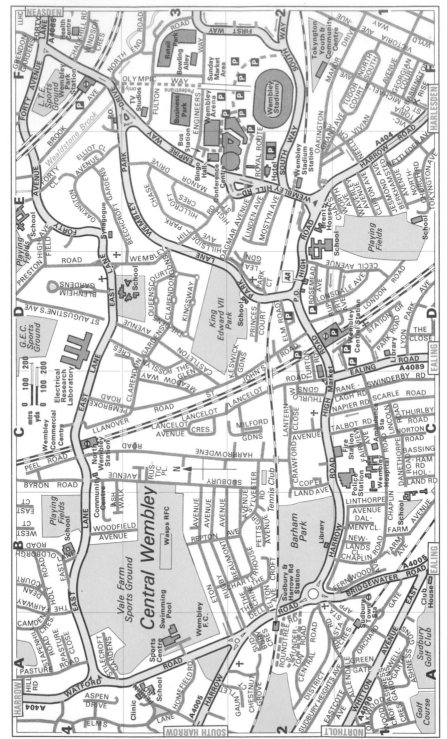

WEST BROMWICH

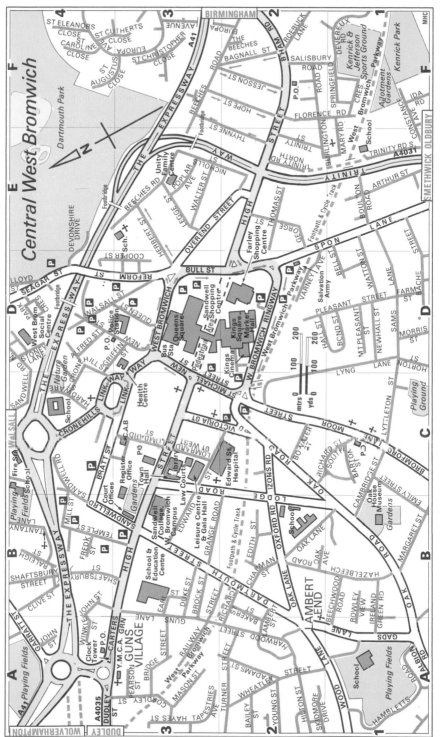

Central West Bromwich

WINCHESTER

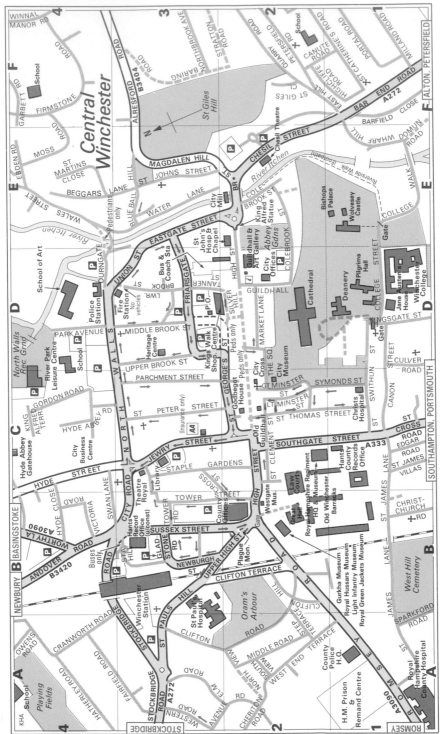

WOKING

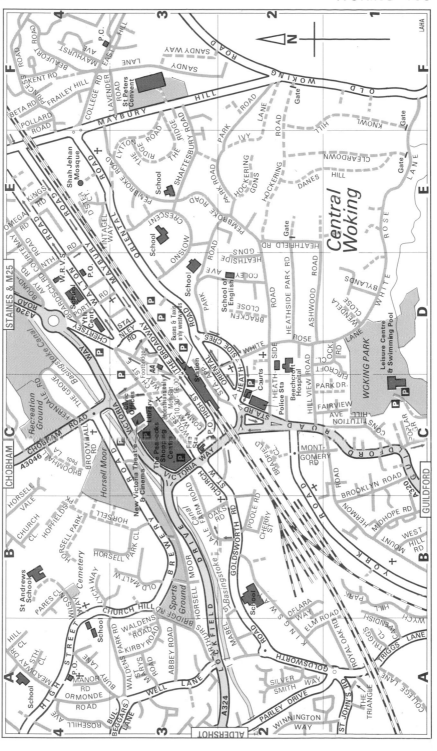

WOLVERHAMPTON

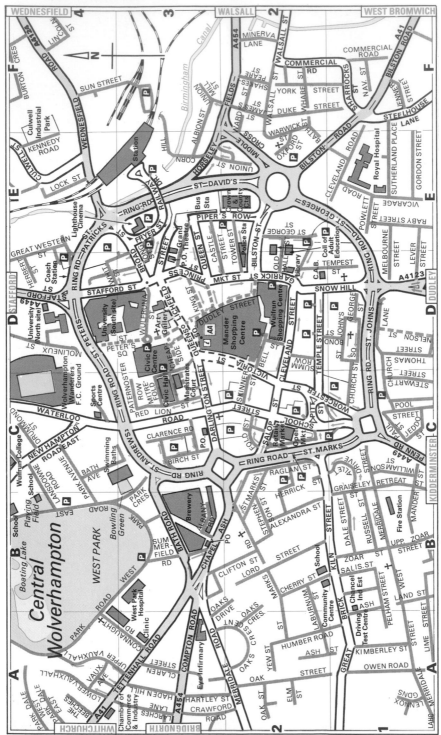

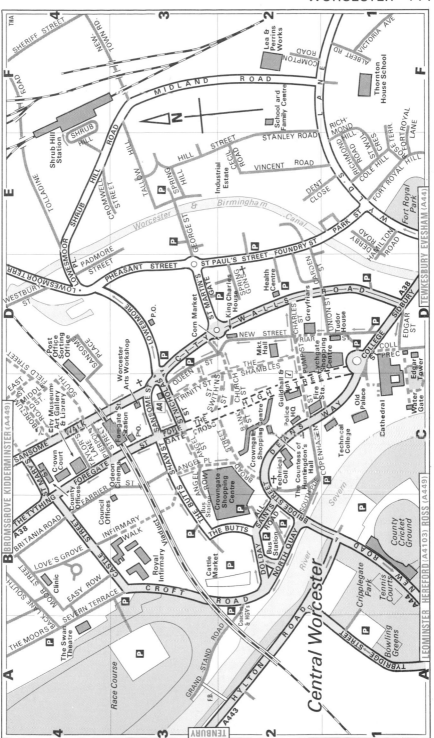

WORCESTER

Central Worcester

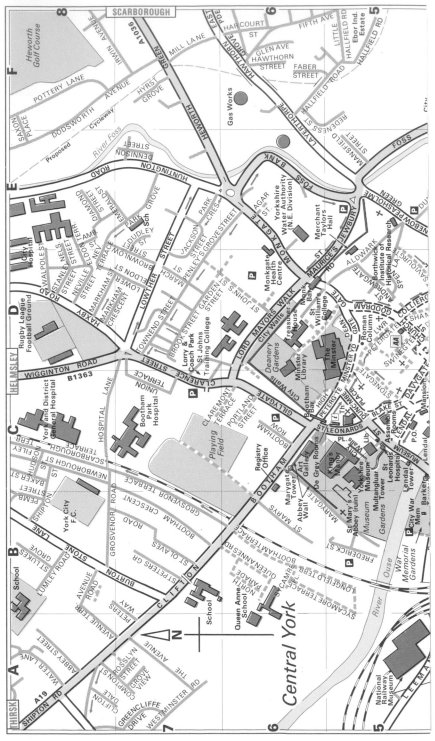

Central York

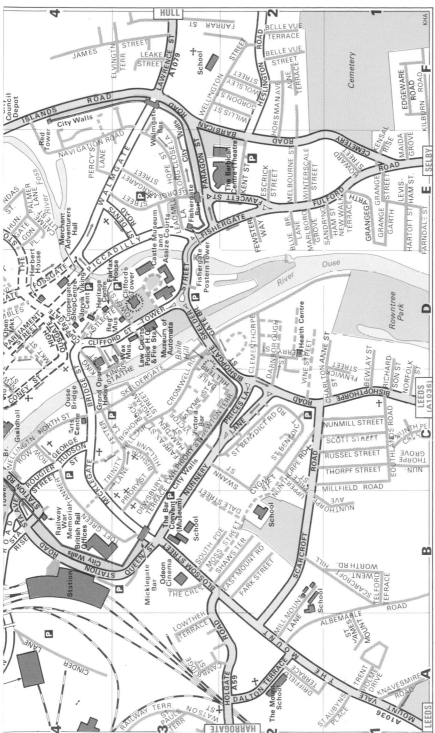

BIRMINGHAM AIRPORT

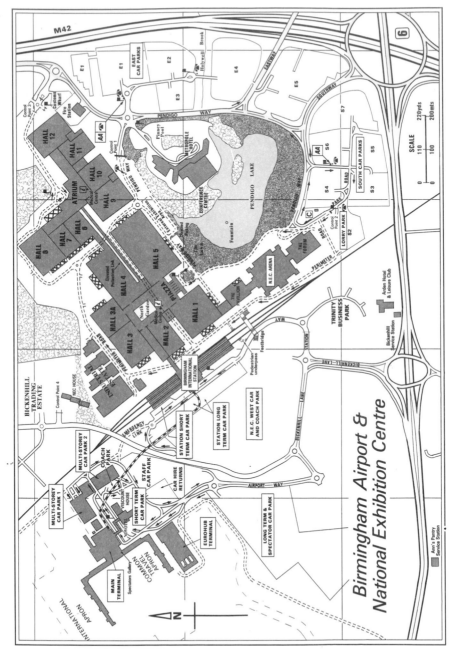

Birmingham Airport &
National Exhibition Centre

EDINBURGH AIRPORT

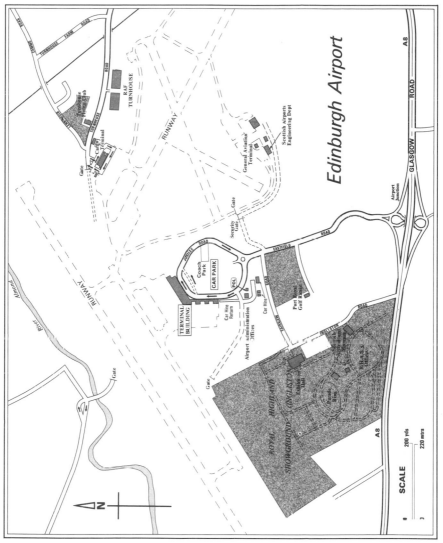

Edinburgh Airport

Turnhouse Flying Club

RAF TURNHOUSE

Cargo Terminal

Gate

RUNWAY

General Aviation Terminal

Scottish Airports Engineering Dept

Security Gate

Gate

JUBILEE ROAD

Coach Park

CAR PARK

POL

TERMINAL BUILDING

Car Hire Return

Airport administration offices

Car Hire

EASTFIELD

EASTFIELD ROAD

Port Royal Golf Range

Gate

INGLISTON

ROYAL HIGHLAND SHOWGROUND (INGLISTON)

Exhibition Hall

Pentland Hall

MacRobert Hall

ROAD

Airport Junction

GLASGOW   ROAD

A8

A8

RUNWAY

River Almond

Gate

TURNHOUSE FARM ROAD

TURNHOUSE ROAD

N

SCALE

200 yds

220 mtrs

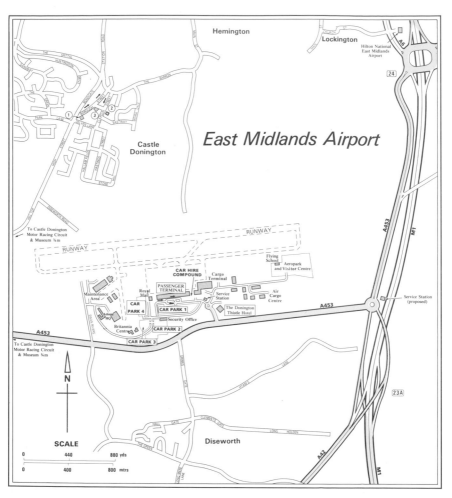

East Midlands Airport

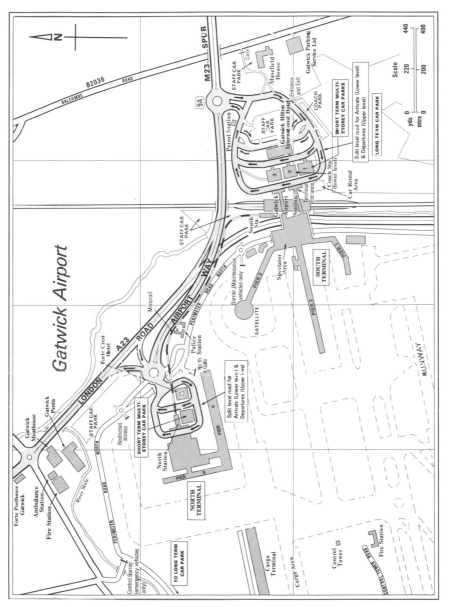

GATWICK AIRPORT

GLASGOW AIRPORT

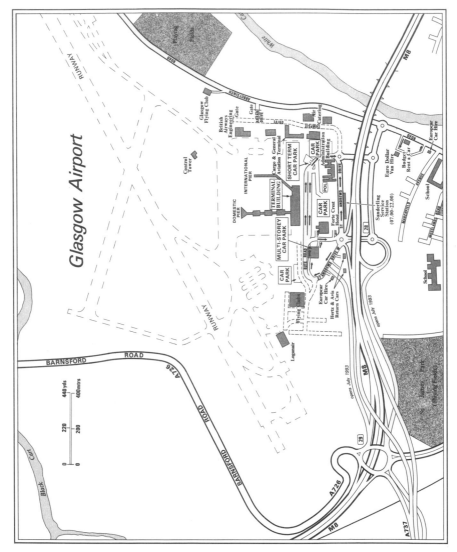

Glasgow Airport

HEATHROW AIRPORT

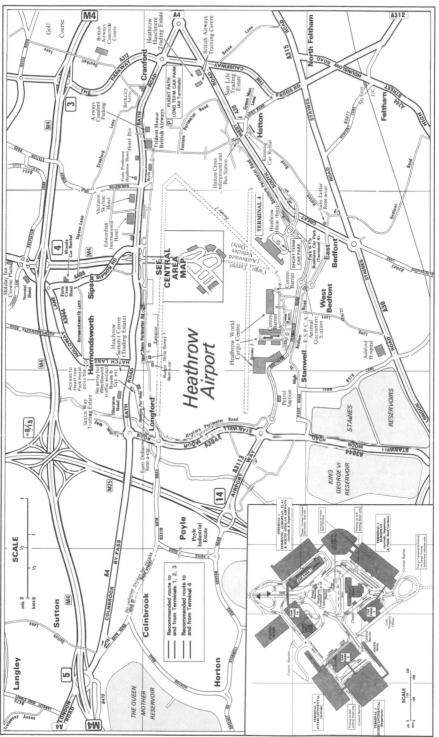

LONDON CITY AIRPORT

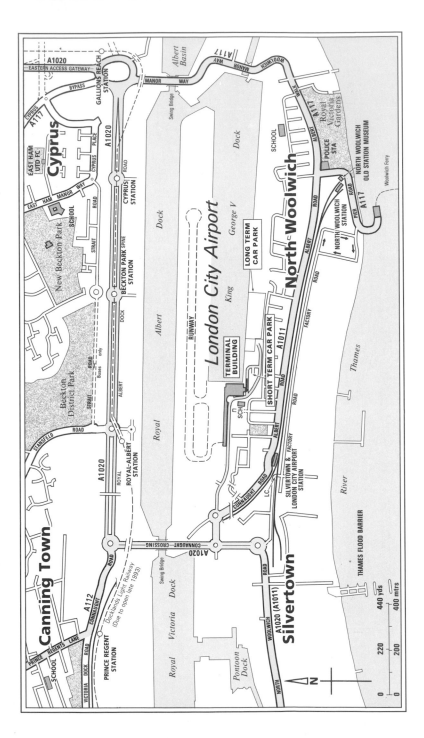

LUTON AIRPORT

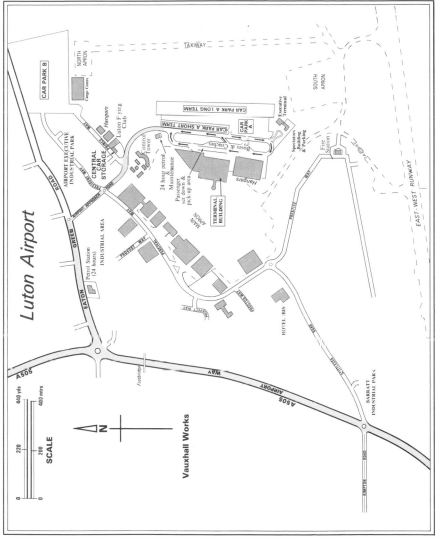

Luton Airport

SCALE

0   220   440 yds

0   200   400 mtrs

N

Vauxhall Works

A505

A505 AIRPORT WAY

KIMPTON ROAD

BARRATT INDUSTRIAL PARK

HOTEL IBIS

BRITISH WAY

PRESTIGE WAY

PERCIVAL WAY

VAUXHALL WAY

OSPREY WAY

SORREL WAY

PROVOST WAY

INDUSTRIAL AREA

Petrol Station (24 hours)

EATON GREEN ROAD

AIRPORT APPROACH ROAD

PRESTIGE WAY

CENTRAL CAR STORAGE

AIRPORT EXECUTIVE INDUSTRIAL PARK

CAR PARK B

NORTH APRON

Cargo Centre

Hangars

Luton Flying Club

Control Tower

24 hour petrol & Maintenance

Passenger set down & pick-up area

TERMINAL BUILDING

MAIN APRON

Hangars

Buses & Coaches

CAR PARK A SHORT TERM

CAR PARK A LONG TERM

CAR PARK A

Spectators Building & Parking

Executive Terminal

SOUTH APRON

Fire Station

TAXIWAY

TAXIWAY

EAST - WEST RUNWAY

Footbridge

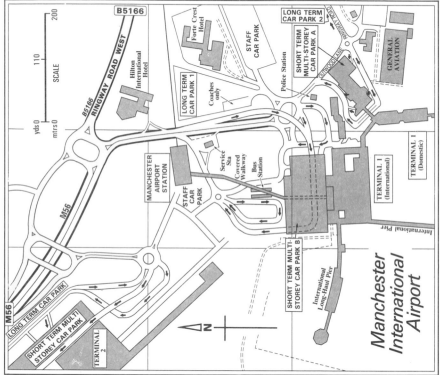

MANCHESTER AIRPORT

STANSTED AIRPORT

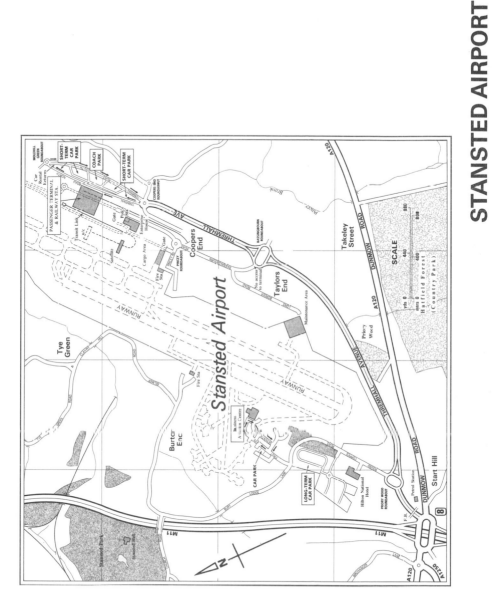

Distance Chart

The distances between towns on the mileage chart are given to the nearest mile, and are measured along the normal AA recommended routes. It should be noted that AA recommended routes do not necessarily follow the shortest distances between places but are based on the quickest travelling time, making maximum use of motorways or dual-carriageway roads.

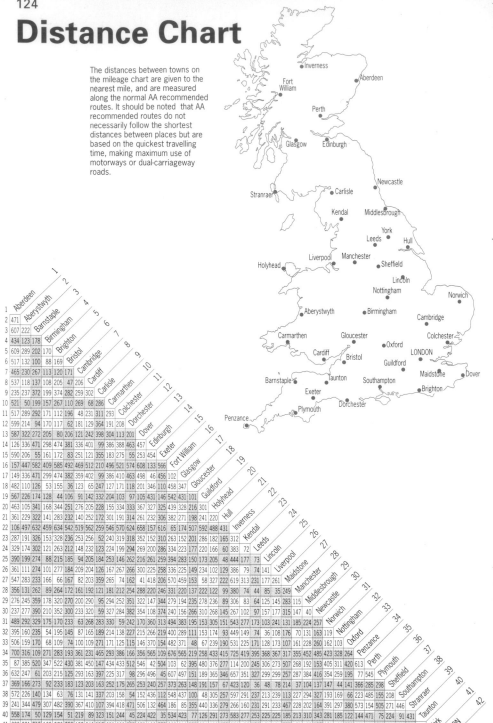